HIRED!

EXPERT ADVICE FROM A LEADING WALL STREET RECRUITER

I0088549

J B   M I L L E R

Hired

Expert Advice
from a leading
**WALL
STREET
RECRUITER**

No matter what industry you are in - if you are looking for
a job today, Hired! will help you get to the front of the line
Head of HR, Financial Firm

COPYRIGHT

!

Copyright © 2012, J.B. Miller.
All rights reserved worldwide.
Published by: TMG Books

No part of this book may be reproduced in any form or by any electronic or mechanical means including information storage and retrieval systems except in the case of brief quotations in articles or reviews without the permission in writing from it's Author, JB Miller.

TMG BOOKS
SAN FRANCISCO

DISCLAIMER

!

The information contained in these materials cannot replace or substitute for the services of trained professionals in any field, including, but not limited to, financial or legal matters. This material is not intended to offer professional legal, medical, personal or financial advice. Under no circumstances will JB Miller, or any of the author's representatives or contractors be liable for any special or consequential damages that result from the use of, or the inability to use, the information or strategies communicated through these materials or any services provided prior to or following the receipt of these materials, even if advised of the possibility of such damages. You alone are responsible and accountable for your decisions, actions and results in life, and by your use of these materials, you agree not to attempt to hold us liable for any such decisions, actions or results, at any time, under any circumstances.

We've taken every effort to ensure we accurately represent these strategies and their potential to help you in your career quest. However, there is no guarantee that you will be successful using the techniques in these materials. Your level of success in attaining results is dependent upon a number of factors including your skill, knowledge, ability, dedication, personality, market, audience, business savvy, business focus, business goals, partners, luck, and financial situation. Because these factors differ according to individuals, we cannot guarantee your success in becoming hired or in your ability to earn revenue, nor can we state that any results suggested in these materials are typical.

Any forward-looking or financial statements outlined here are simply illustrative and not promises for actual performance. These statements and the strategies offered in these materials are simply our opinion or experience. So again, as stipulated by law, no future guarantees can be made that you will achieve any results or income from our information and we offer no professional legal or financial advice. Identities and locations of companies and individuals in this book have been changed to protect their privacy. Any resemblance between persons cited in this book and specific persons the reader might know or recognize are coincidental only.

COPYRIGHT © 2012, JB MILLER

DEDICATION

!

*"To all of the job seekers in the world who are
serious about securing their Dream Job"*

*The goal of HIRED! is to get 10,000,000 people
worldwide back to work and into the
job of their dreams*

Table Of Contents

!

ACKNOWLEDGEMENTS

!

Enormous thanks to my family for supporting me during the writing of HIRED! They get the gold heart award for putting up with my late nights and 'do not disturb' signs affixed to my home office door as I scribed this book, sometimes into the wee morning hours. I am grateful for their love, laughter and an occasional unsolicited snack placed quietly nearby.

They know how passionate I am about helping to reduce the unemployment rate in our country and my secret goal of getting 10,000,000 people worldwide back to work.

Thank you to my editor who always gave me concrete and constructive advice with a positive tone throughout this process.

And most of all, thank you to you, the reader, for committing to make your career life the best it can be.

– JB Miller

WHY YOU NEED THIS BOOK

!

YOU ARE READY TO FIND YOUR DREAM JOB

HIRED! accompanies you beyond just getting a job. It encourages you to follow the steps in this book in order to secure your *dream job*. This book will help you find what inspires you and where your passion lies. So if this is what you want, then you have chosen the right book. This book will show you how to take control of your future. It is written for you.

YOU ARE HAPPY AND SECURE IN YOUR CURRENT POSITION

You may be happy with your current employment and think that this book is not for you, but I am here to tell you - it is! Why? Because, quite frankly, when it comes to job security today, the world has changed. Even if you are happy in your current role, are doing a stellar job and are receiving all of the right reviews and accolades, you could face changes beyond your control.

- Your company may need to cut expenses to increase profits

- A new management team may come in and want their own people on board
- A new hire may be in line for your job
- You may be too expensive
- You may not be political enough
- You may be part of *out with the old and in with the new*
- You may not get paid what you are expecting because you are tied to company performance, which may lead to unhappiness or a change in your employment

There are many reasons that you may be *let go* and I am here to tell you that while you need not live a paranoid life, you should never be satisfied with the status quo. You must always be open to change and view change as opportunity.

We live in a *loyal-less society*™ and you must be sure that *you* are loyal to your dreams and desires. You may not need some of the ideas in this book today, but you need to be ready in case you find yourself out of work tomorrow!

YOU ARE DEPRESSED BECAUSE YOU CAN'T FIND A JOB

This book is for you right now! Don't wait to read it. It will help get you out of your depression (unless, of course, you are naturally or chemically depressed - then you should see your doctor) and it will motivate you to get HIRED!

If you have been FIRED - depression, lack of self-esteem and even a fear of trying are common by products. You are not unusual and you are not alone. This book will help you map out your plan to not only getting *a* job, but also ultimately getting your Dream Job! It will take discipline and commitment, but once you get started you will be amazed at how energized and motivated you will feel.

If you are *in it to win it*, then this book is for you.

YOU WANT CONCISE, HOW-TO INFORMATION – FAST!

HIRED! is not filled with fluff or hyperbole. It has been condensed to give you the essentials. The chapters are purposefully short so that you can use HIRED! as a quick reference. Consult it often. Keep it nearby so that you can refer to it as you would a trusted guide.

HIRED! contains sources of BONUS resources by way of QR codes and links throughout. For the QR codes, all you need to do is scan each code with your smartphone and you will access the BONUS material immediately. Search for and download the QR READER app from your smartphone app store – it's free. This book also contains many URL's to additional online resources that we support and that you can access as often as you would like. Just plug the address into your computer browser and you will have instant access.

On the www.hiredsecrets.com website, you are invited to submit your name and email to receive ongoing job seeking tips on a real time basis. These tips, tricks and strategies are free and take into account the newest trends in recruiting and job search.

My goal is to keep you current, regardless of what phase you are in in your quest for your Dream Job. It will be up to you to use these techniques and strategies. It is my ongoing gift to you in keeping my promise that I will do all I can to help you secure your Dream Job!

YOU ARE A HIRING MANAGER

You may think you do not need this book because you are the one in the driver's seat. It is you who does the hiring. Don't be complacent. Human resources people get 'RIF'd' all of the time and the next one could be you. Maybe you are the Head of HR - at the top of your profession. You may be too expensive or need to make way for the younger generation who are so tech savvy it would scare you. The world of hiring in general has also changed and this book will help you keep on top of tools and resources that can help you hire the best talent possible for your company's openings, as well as prepare you for any changes you may personally encounter.

YOU ARE A RECRUITER

You may think that this book is not for you because you already know how to find and place talented people. You might want to reconsider because in HIRED! you will find many tips on sourcing talent, just as talent learns how to find you. There is even a special chapter just for you!

Welcome Aboard!

Publisher Foreword

!

In HIRED!, you will find the information you need to seek out and secure your dream job. The philosophy in this book is organized to address psychological readiness as well as practical application.

The Author of this book has had successful careers in the industries of media, strategic consulting and finance and is a highly respected Wall Street Recruiter. The Author has seen every sort of hiring situation and has placed talented people in leading positions.

This book contains examples of job seekers who have applied the principles in this book and have met with success. It tells you how you can meet with success in your job quest too. Take from this book the ideas that speak to you. You may only need one or two, or all of them, depending on what stage you are in as it relates to your job search. Study this book; it will help you where you stand today and it will guide you to where you ultimately want to be.

Hired! will give you the confidence and inspiration that you need to believe in yourself and to take the necessary steps to attain your goal. It will show you how. All who read and absorb this book will be ahead of the hiring game and on their way to securing the job of their dreams.

FROM THE AUTHOR

!

Thank you for purchasing HIRED!

HIRED! was written to give you, the job seeker, expert advice based on my years of experience as an Executive Recruiter. I want you to secure your dream job - quickly. No matter what industry you are in or aspire to be in, in HIRED! you will be guided with practical, applicable, no nonsense advice so that you can put your best foot forward - and get HIRED!

For Hiring Managers and Recruiters, there is a special chapter just for you so that you can get a leg up on the competition for talent. Welcome to you as well!

I think of myself as a renaissance person. I thrive on being open-minded and have always followed my occupational and creative goals with fervour. My journey thus far has been nothing short of varied, exciting and rewarding. My career path has included: Television Advertising Executive for a leading National Television Network, Television Producer, Strategic Consultant to Fortune 100-500 Corporations, Board Member, Non-Profit Co-Founder, Investment Banker, and the career that all of my previous positions have prepared me for - Executive Recruiter.

I have worked in Manhattan, San Francisco and San Luis Obispo. I have travelled to most states in the United States, throughout the Caribbean, every Northern European Country and Israel.

Throughout my varied career I have worked 100-hour weeks and 20-hour weeks. I have enlisted the help of nannies, babysitters, au pairs and my own mother (not advised!).

I have spoken and met with thousands of jobseekers from every walk of life and have placed many motivated people like you in wonderful jobs where they continue to thrive.

I respect everyone along the hiring food chain. Whether they are the junior Human Resources person at a technology company or the CEO of an Investment Bank, I believe that each person I come into contact with has something valuable to offer.

I am comfortable with candidates who have graduated from the Ivy League or those who have no college education at all.

Finally, I consider myself a Life Coach first and foremost and I am going to help you get on track to securing your dream job! It is very rewarding for me to see deserving people get HIRED! I know you are one of them.

So let's get started!

- J.B. Miller

*"Success requires no apologies,
failure permits no alibis"*

- Copernicus

INTRODUCTION

!

We live in interesting times.

As I write this book, the U.S. Bureau of Labour
Statistics places unemployment at just below 8.0%,
or 12,100,000 out of work. The unemployment rate
had been above 8% for more than 40 months. While
this dip may be encouraging, according to a recent
CNBC report, the national average could actually be
closer to 15% - almost double that of current
estimates.

From 1948 through 2010 unemployment averaged
out to 5.7%. Some years were much higher (early
80s) and others were much lower (late 70s, late 80s).
As of today, long-term employment (which means
people looking for work for more than six months)
is 40%. The reality is - the longer you are
unemployed, the harder it is to get a job. Some
states are even exploring legislation that makes it
illegal to NOT consider someone for a position just
because they are out of work.

Our country is in turmoil, but not as tumultuous as
when unemployment reached almost 11% in the
early 80s. The good news is that the world of
unemployment has peaks and valleys. The bad news
is that we are at a pretty high unemployment peak
right now - and there is no relief in sight.

The United States has become an integral part of the global economy, tied to most countries in a co-dependent manner. Whether we are suppliers of goods and services, borrowers of money or importers of other nation's stuff, when other countries suffer, we suffer too. Think of Greece, Spain, Italy and several others.

Add in the cost of our wars and other countries wars, the mortgage melt down, rise in food and retail goods (while packaging and quality contracts), repeated jumps in healthcare costs and the high price of travel, and you get companies cutting corners. We are being nickel and dimed everywhere today. From airplane baggage fees and early check in fees to withdrawing our own money, we are personally experiencing the reality that corporations need to show quarterly profits. What do we get as a result of this on-going pressure to perform? Cuts – 'reduction in force.' People get FIRED!

Welcome to what I refer to as the *LOYAL-LESS SOCIETY* ™.

Employers can no longer afford to reward dedicated employees. Gone are the days where people like my Uncle stay with the same company for their ENTIRE CAREER! My Uncle rose up to CEO of a large industrial public company and became the second largest shareholder before he retired. My Grandfather wasn't much different. He worked for the same energy company his entire life and received a pension until the day he died. Wow! A pension! There aren't too many of those left either.

People are angry. They are angry at everything. The government, the local grocer, the school boards, even the solicitors that knock on their doors. Yet it seems that as of late, people are mostly angry with WALL STREET.

While much of the frustration over TARP money and big bonuses can make a person's blood boil, I am here to tell you that working on Wall Street is not always 'all that' as they say.

Yes, there are heavy hitters and rain makers that make the big bucks, but I'll bet you weren't aware that many of the 'suits' you see flooding into your cities financial districts are working for FREE! That's right, there are many financial executives who are on 100% commission! Several even pay their own office rent, marketing expenses, healthcare and T&E (Travel and Entertainment). They do this with the hopes that they will 'close a deal' or convince some wealthy individual or institution to adhere to their financial advice, resulting in a handsome fee.

If you have been following the news, you will notice that the cash component of Wall Street bonuses at some of the biggest global banks is getting smaller and the stock component is getting deferred out for many years. Stringent parameters are being put into place around vesting and giving back based on company performance. In almost every call I have with Investment Bankers, they inevitably ask me how I can help them get *out* of the business!

I have a neighbour who is working under the 'eat what you kill' model. He has a kid that is into a sport that requires hundreds of dollars of coaching a week, as well as tournament costs every weekend. He has a vacation home in the mountains that he can't sell and his wife is in bad health. He goes into the office every day and has a 'kitchen table deal' with his employer. Basically, an office, a desk, a phone and a firm to hang his license on. His salary? $0.00.

I know an Investment Banker with four kids who can't pay his mortgage. He was fired when new management came in with a new team and after the shell shock wore off, he spent the next six months interviewing with every firm in his city. When he and I finally connected, we had several heart to heart talks about what he really wanted to do, and what he realized was that he was an entrepreneur at heart. He recently went on to run a company in the food business that helps entrepreneurs get their products made, packaged, labelled, marketed and onto store shelves. He could not be happier and he has stock in the company, which could lead to a nice exit down the road.

I know a senior manager at a leading energy company who was an Investment Banker for many years (at top firms). He had a heart attack in his early 30s. Yes, the job is stressful! Now, in his new job, he gets a regular paycheck, has a say in company policy and direction, and is happy with a consistent and predictable life.

Many jobs on Wall Street are not unlike being a car salesman who says *buy my nice car, it's better than the other guy's*. Trust me when I tell you that many finance professionals are thinking that selling cars might be the way to go! So before you blame everyone in the financial markets for your personal situation, thinking they are all rich and crooked and are getting theirs while you are not, you must take a deep breath and know that everything is not always as it seems.

In HIRED! I am not here to defend Wall Street; there are many elements that are simply indefensible. But I *am* here to encourage you to look beyond your anger, disappointment or frustration with those around you, and instead, focus within and on your particular plan for success. Don't waste your time being angry. It's time to do something that you will benefit from. After all, that is what really matters - who you are, where you want to go and how you are going to get there.

I am here to take you down the path to figuring out what you really want in life and how to get it. You will learn about others like you and how they got HIRED! by using the advice and strategies in this book.

Whether you are unemployed and have been looking for work (for too long maybe) or you are gainfully employed, yet miserable in your job for any number of reasons, HIRED! is designed to help you.

I know an employee who worked 120-hour weeks and only saw his son for 1/2 hour a day. That's it. He made good money, but he was miserable - it was time for him to make a major change. He agreed that being more of a big fish in a slightly smaller pond would not only increase his status at the new firm (and the firm would benefit from his background), but he would also not have to travel as much *and* would get to spend quality time with his wife and child. Moneywise, he received a better formula for upside potential and became part of the senior strategy team. It was a winning scenario for everyone.

I know a caregiver who has been out of work for over a year and living on unemployment. According to the Employment Security Department, here are the rules: People who collect unemployment must be *able* to work, *available* for work and *actively seeking* suitable work. They must verify that they are meeting these requirements by filing a claim each week. That must be pretty exhausting. Better she finds a job. This book is just as much for her as it is for the employee making lots of money but who is miserable.

I know another job seeker who was fired from his job managing a restaurant chain location. He did something stupid out of concern for an employee and it cost him his job. He can't get hired again in food service. This book is for people like him who need to re-invent themselves.

I know another job seeker who decided to leave the world of corporate politics to 'do his own thing.' This book is for him as well, to show him how to navigate that change.

In HIRED! you will learn how to clarify your career aspirations. You will receive life coaching advice and strategies as well as sure-fire tactics, tips and resources that will help you get out in front of the competition and get HIRED!

BELIEF

In order to be successful in your quest, you must believe that you deserve to get hired, and furthermore, to have the job of your dreams. We all have the right to achieve our highest aims. Belief in yourself and your own ability to meet your goals (no matter how lofty) will be crucial to your success in obtaining your dream job.

When I was working at a media firm in NYC, I attended a major industry event at the famous Plaza Hotel. Huddled in the middle of the elaborate ballroom were the CEO of a major television network (and all of its holdings), the President of the network and a key member of the SEC

(Securities and Exchange Commission) who helped set the ceiling as to how many individual television stations any one network could own in any one market. Right there, in front of several hundred people, stood three industry icons and two cameramen filming their laughter and backslapping. They were celebrities in the world of business media. As I took my place along the edge, what I found most interesting was that no one seemed to have the courage to advance toward the men. Not a single person moved. Well that was about to change.

I looked at the person I had brought to the event, took a deep breath and approached the group. "Hello Mr. CEO, I'm JB Miller," I said as I extended my hand. "I work for XYZ, but I plan to work for you at your television network very soon."

Well, that's all it took. The CEO shook my hand and introduced me to the President, who, in turn, introduced me to the SEC Commissioner. For the next minute or so, it was the cameramen and the four of us holding court in the middle of a sea of spectators.

That particular moment in time took all of the courage I could muster and resulted in not only one of the most inspirational experiences I had ever had, it was the impetuous to what would become, at the time, my dream job. I still remember how nervous I was, yet more importantly, how determined I was to meet the group. I faced my fear head on and with determination at my side; I conquered the moment and set my path on a new course.

My boldness must have broken the ice because shortly thereafter, everyone in the room converged upon the icons, at which point I quietly slipped away and back to my guest.

The best part of the story was that three months later, I was working for that very same television network. Not because I had met the CEO, President and a powerful political figure, but because I had the courage, determination and perseverance to follow my dreams and reach for what was *my* dream job at that point in my life. You can do it too and I am here to help you.

LET'S TALK ABOUT YOUR

SPECIFIC SITUATION

This book is written for you and I most definitely wish to hear from you. I invite you to share your success stories with me as you implement the strategies in this book. I will be highlighting certain success stories on my website and in interviews. Names will be kept confidential. Please feel free to email the details of your story to me at info@hiredsecrets.com. I look forward to connecting with you.

Finally, if it is your cover letter or résumé that you need help with, you can order my personal Critique

Services. Just plug this link into your browser and we'll get started.

http://sellfy.com/p/q3hd

Are you ready to take your first step toward success?

Welcome to HIRED!

ONE - SECRETS FOR SUCCESS

!

READINESS

Before you begin your dream job journey, you must take inventory of your readiness. What is your state of mind? Are you scared, discouraged - defeated before you start? Do you lack self-confidence? Or are you jazzed, pumped up and ready to act? Are you determined to make a change or are you terrified to? Wherever you are at emotionally, recognize it and know that it is OK.

You bought this book because you want to find your dream job. If you are uncertain or shy about starting, the best remedy is to decide that you are going to act. If you don't feel completely prepared to go after the job of your dreams, that's OK. The answers you require will come to you along the way.

The key is to start. Start now. Start today. By purchasing this book you are, indeed, starting on your journey to finding and securing your dream job. Read this book and gain knowledge that will give you confidence, understanding and perseverance.

Trust your instincts. Listen to your inner voice. You know more than you give yourself credit for.

RESOLUTION

If you are going to be successful in your job quest, you first need to decide what your dream job is. Once you have read HIRED!, answered the self assessment questions, done your research and determined what it is that you want, then you must stay firm with your choice and believe that you will get it. Be resolute in your decision and see it through. Do not waver and do not change your mind if your first attempt is not successful.

See yourself in your new job. Use your senses to experience the new world around you. Bask in your success. Do this for a short span each day and soon you will be so motivated that you will be showing others how to move forward with their lives too!

ORGANIZATION

Once you have made your choice, it will be time to organize your efforts so that you develop a solid path to job success. This book shows you how.

HAVE FAITH

Life is filled with ups and downs. The person who prevails is the one that enjoys the ups and when he experiences the downs, he learns from them and creates a new plan toward success. You must have faith in the process. Be confident. Be persistent, no matter how many times you may stumble. Often it is the grandest successes that occur right after a fall.

At one year old, my eldest could not walk. He crawled by dragging his left leg and his floppy body tone required support so that he could sit up. When he spoke the few words that he had, it was only in vowels.

We took him to a renowned Pediatric Neurologist who, after examining him, informed us in no uncertain terms that the boy would be ½ of his life behind. While the news stunned and upset his father and me, it was at that moment that I decided that our son would have a normal life.

As he grew, he continued to speak in vowels, which made his desires hard to understand for those outside of the family. It was suggested during his first IEP (Individual Educational Plan) meeting that he be put into a Special Education program in another town, where he could be with children similar to him. I wouldn't have it. Through sheer determination and faith, we kept our son in the regular school system and arranged for him to have break out services to address his affliction. We sent him to daily speech and occupational therapy lessons and refused to have him learn sign language. He would speak. That was, quite clearly, the decision we had made for him.

My son is 20 now. He has gone through regular schooling with special classes within the mainstream environment and can speak clearly. He is currently attending our local Community College in an adaptive program, has a part-time job and lives in a high functioning group facility a few miles from home. While his thoughts and desires are simple, he is confident in himself, has become a contributing member to our community and he is happy.

It took many years of faith to endure the constant opposition from school officials and regular reminders of what my son couldn't do, to enable me to stay the course and be a steadfast advocate for him.

As you embark on your job search, you must have faith in yourself, regardless of what others say. Know that you can achieve that to which you desire. You may need to try many times, yet do not lose faith in your attempts. It is unyielding faith that will carry you on to success.

SUPPORT

Surround yourself with positive and supportive people. Do not listen to those that discourage or criticize you. Often these are family members or even close friends, so be cautious when you seek outside council.

PERSIST

Persistence, above all, is the one characteristic that will lead to success. No matter how you may feel on a particular day, no matter how many times you may stumble, pick yourself up and go forward. Do something toward your goal every day. You will prevail. I know this from experience.

One of the mantras that I live by is *finish the task at hand*. When I want to quit, I don't. Why - because I have to finish the task at hand. I know that every small task that I complete adds up to the accomplishment of the big task, the big goal, the whopping success! You can do this too. Persist at all costs until you have met your goal.

Once you get into the habit of completing tasks that get you closer to your dream job, you will find that you don't have enough time in the day to do all that you want to do.

Great things are about to happen for you with your career. I can feel it. You are on your way to the most successful life you could have ever imagined.

ONE REVIEW

!

- ① ASSESS YOUR EMOTIONAL STATE

- ① DECIDE WHAT YOU WANT AND BEGIN, REGARDLESS IF YOU ARE FULLY READY

- ① ACTION REPLACES PROCRASTINATION

- ① IGNORE NEGATIVE INFLUENCES

- ① PERSISTENCE EQUALS SUCCESS

TWO– DEFINING YOUR DREAM JOB

!

Are you in a job where you are content but you have an irking feeling that it is not what you were put on this earth for? Are you no longer intellectually challenged in your current position and just know that there is something more meaningful out there?

Maybe you have been displaced and before you jump at the first thing that comes through the door, you have a little time to figure out what the heck your dream job is.

When I was working in television advertising, I was fascinated with the tan box that dominated my assistant's desk. There she would sit, day after day, staring at a dark gray screen with green letters that appeared as her fingers clicked away on a crude typewriter looking keyboard. I did not have one of those boxes on my desk and was curious as to its value. I soon learned that the box was a dedicated computer that linked television station's commercial ordering systems to our office in Manhattan. When I brought in a paper order, my assistant would input the information into the box and off it would go (via dial-up) to a television station in Montgomery, Alabama or Roanoke, Virginia.

You may have already guessed that this was before computers were officially born into mainstream society. The closest thing to a computer that I knew of at the time was a 'personal organizer' that all of the top brass at my company owned. Basically, it was a calendar and contact depository, not much more.

After spending several years in television advertising (*spots and dots* as we called it), I stopped being intellectually challenged – I got bored. On the hour-long train ride home from Manhattan to Connecticut each day, I pondered my life (there were no cell phones, laptops or tablets to distract me). What exactly was it that I did in my daily work life? Basically, I wined and dined media buyers in hopes that they would spend their client's advertising dollars on the television stations whose inventory I represented. I put together packages and incentives, and combined ratings in creative ways to convince the 'media queens' (as they were fondly referred) that my stable of programs fell into their requirements. But really – my job was nothing short of bribing. I was good at it. I showed up with jewelry, tickets to sporting events and Broadway plays, dinner certificates, trips, whatever it took to get the order. Well, not whatever, but if it didn't cost too much and if I could put it on my expense account, I gifted it. Buying gifts and packaging commercials wasn't exactly what I had in mind for my ultimate career. I found myself asking - is this what my life is all about - buy me, bring me, take me? Was I using any of my brainpower at all? Is this what I would do for the rest of my adult career existence? I couldn't stand it anymore! And as for the tan box, I found myself drifting back to it and imagining its potential. As fate would have it, my husband was offered a position at an excellent firm in San Francisco, and so we 'up and left' New York City to start our new lives on the West Coast.

While searching for a home for our growing family, I had more time to dream of what my dream job might be. I went on long walks and asked myself many of the assessment questions that I encourage you to consider. I suggest that you answer the questions honestly. After all, this process is for you and you alone, so the more real you can be with yourself, the more likely you will discover that which you are meant to do.

I continued with my probing inquiry, unaware of the fact that my mind kept drifting back to the square tan box. I talked about the box to friends and my husband and imagined a way that my old job in spots and dots could be migrated to a more sophisticated process. One day as I was walking my two children along the water's edge in Tiburon, bam! I knew what I was meant to do. I would create an electronic negotiating system for the sale of television airtime. Of course! I knew how the interpersonal process worked, how television program ratings were analyzed (based off of Nielsen and Arbitron) and I knew people at every step of the transaction chain.

The bottom line is that I made a promise to myself at that moment that I would be the next CEO of a leading software company. Little did I know that my idea was being formed way before the likes of EBay!

Once I had made my decision, I let myself get very excited about it and often visualized myself sitting at the head of a conference table in front of my Board of Directors as I brought them up to speed on the success of my venture. I let my imagination wander and envisioned my success at every turn.

That's when things began to fall into place. I was so hyper aware of my purpose that I began to notice and take advantage of opportunity as it presented itself to me. It was as though the world had opened its door just to bring me what I needed to succeed in my venture.

I made a list of who I knew. The week before we moved to California, I had had dinner at the home of one of the industries most ruthless purchasers of television airtime on behalf of some of the world's largest advertisers. I would ask that firm to be my test market on the buy side. I knew the owners of more than 25 television stations and knew I could convince one of them to test my solution on the sell side. I had met a computer programmer at the last NAB Convention (National Association of Broadcasters) that I had attended and hired him to do the initial screens. I talked to the head of sales at a local San Francisco television station and found out the name of the firm that programmed their sales system. I met with the firm and they agreed to develop the entire system in exchange for a small percentage of equity. I met a leading corporate attorney on a plane ride to Los Angeles and he became the first member of my board. It went on from there.

My point in telling you this is that I gave myself time to dream of what I really wanted to do and once I had decided what it was (regardless of the fact that I had no idea how I would do it), I started to move forward. By answering the following questions, my hope is that they help you to come a step or more closer to figuring out what your dream job might be.

PERSONAL ASSESSMENT QUESTIONS

1. Are you happy in your current role or were you happy before you were let go?
2. Is their/was their upside potential?
3. Do you/did you like going to work?
4. What do you like/dislike about your current (or most recent) job?

5. Do you/did you feel at all intellectually challenged in your position?
6. Do you/did you feel smarter than everyone else?
7. Are you/were you advancing your skills in your current/recent role?
8. What have you/did you accomplish in your role?
9. What do you/did you like the most about your position? Travel? Entertaining? Power? Intellectually challenging? Etc.
10. What is important to you? Money, time, travel, flexibility, advancement, power.
11. How do you feel (did you feel) when you achieve (d) a goal?
12. Why do you want to make a change? Career Advancement? Money? Usefulness? Interest?
13. What are the best parts of your personality?
14. What are you most criticized for? Have you considered changing that trait?
15. Do you take responsibility for your actions or do you blame others?
16. Are you jealous of those more successful than you or are you motivated to better your station?
17. Do you surround yourself with negative or positive people?
18. Do you give yourself time to just think, dream and ponder?
19. What are your favorite activities or hobbies?

20. How do you feel when you are doing them?
21. What kind of job do you think would help to replicate those good feelings?
22. How do you add value?
23. What have you done in the last year where you were so involved that you lost track of time? This is one of the most important questions you can ask yourself for this will unveil your passion.
24. Do you take time to be alone?
25. What enters your mind when you let your imagination wander?
26. What kind of books, stories do you like to read? What kind of movies do you like to watch?
27. What gives you the biggest rush?
28. What gives you the biggest smile and sense of peace?
29. Are you yourself in your job (current or past)?
30. When are you most yourself?

These are the types of questions that I asked myself and continue to ask myself on a regular basis. I hope you will take the time to ponder them. I believe that in answering them honestly, you will get closer to understanding what your dream job should be. It might be in an entirely new industry or it may be in your current field doing something different.

Remember my story about the software company? No, I didn't get funded. Why? In the end, I was not being completely true to myself and deep down I knew it. I ended up taking on a partner who had no understanding of the television advertising business. Secretly I wanted the assistance of her well-known relative who worked for a prestigious law firm. I should have simply asked him to help me. Instead, I agreed to bring on his family member as my marketing partner. The problem was, whenever we went to meetings she sat silent. Why? Because she had no idea what the industry was about. I did my best to bring her up to speed but ultimately the choice of a partnership was my demise. I was also insecure at the time about my ability to succeed on my own at such a tremendous undertaking. As a result, I wanted someone to come along for the ride. That was also a mistake for I had everything I needed laid out in front of me and I believe that the right alliance would have presented itself, either via my Board of Directors that I had compiled or via clients using my solution.

The good news is that my experience starting a company led to my work as a high level strategic consultant for a number of Fortune 100-500 corporations who paid me very well for my market perspective. One of those companies was developing their own trading platform for a different industry and I was able to offer my advice. I continued on my journey and found that I loved consulting. I enjoyed the periodic travel, providing value with my knowledge and being handsomely paid. That experience led to my becoming an Investment Banker, which took my understanding of industry, growth strategy and alliances to a level where I began putting companies together. And then, after several years as an Investment Banker, I decided to reduce the travel and 120 hour weeks so that I could spend more time with my family. Voila! My position as Founder and President of an Executive Search firm was born! I love what I do and I find great satisfaction in helping talented people like you find their dream job. I have found mine. Now it's time for you to find yours!

Life is a journey and a journey is to be embarked upon. So regardless of where you are in your occupational life cycle, my advice is to begin the process now - today. You may not have enough money to make a change. You may be scared to make a change. You may be desperate to make a change. Studies have shown that people change careers 5-7 times in their lifetime (nowadays it is even more). We live in a loyal-less society yet you are obligated to be loyal to yourself in order to achieve your quest of obtaining your dream job.

FORMAL ASSESSMENTS

Other more formal assessments to help you narrow your dream job focus include personality and/or career analysis tests where in you answer questions about your preferences and approach to situations. The test spits out personality traits to guide you and/or career suggestions to spark your desire.

Here are links to some of those tests:

http://www.careerpath.com

http://www.myersbriggs.org

http://www.whatcareerisrightforme.com

http://similarminds.com/personality_tests.html

http://www.humanmetrics.com/cgi-win/jtypes2.asp

The personality and career assessment tests are designed to help you zero in on those characteristics and personality traits that will bring you the greatest match in terms of industry and job category.

I believe that down deep we all know what it is that we are meant to do. Maybe we are working in a desk job and secretly wish to be a musician. Why not work for a production company and learn about producing music while working on your own tunes?

Maybe you are a travelling salesman and all you want to do is work with animals instead of people. You might be happier putting your skills to work selling a product that helps farm animals stay healthy or race horses train more efficiently. You also may enjoy volunteering at your local Humane Society.

A SIDE NOTE ABOUT TESTS

PRE-EMPLOYMENT TESTS

When you interview for a new position, it is quite possible that you will be given a test to determine your compatibility with company culture or firm requirements. Tests can include blood or urine samples, team player analysis, and psychological suitability tests. Many of these tests ask you questions where-in your answer choices may be 'strongly agree,' 'agree,' 'disagree,' 'strongly disagree' or 'neutral' about a particular posed scenario. Don't try to figure out the answer that the test wants. They ask the same question in many different ways to adjust for this possibility. Just be honest. Always.

Here is one test you do not want to pass!

Have you ever read the book *The Psychopath Test* by Jon Ronson? It is about how many leaders throughout our history could, in fact, be deemed psychopaths due to their extreme narcissistic and predatory behavior. It is an interesting read. Here are some of the key characteristics to determine if you are one! A word of caution: just because you may meet some of the characteristics, you need to match all of them to be considered a psychopath!

The twenty traits assessed by the PCL-R score are:

- Glib and superficial charm
- Grandiose (exaggeratedly high) estimation of self
- Need for stimulation
- Pathological lying
- Cunning and manipulativeness
- Lack of remorse or guilt
- Shallow affect
- Superficial emotional responsiveness)
- Callousness and lack of empathy
- Parasitic lifestyle
- Poor behavioral controls
- Sexual promiscuity
- Early behavior problems
- Lack of realistic long-term goals
- Impulsivity
- Irresponsibility
- Failure to accept responsibility for own actions
- Many short-term marital relationships
- Juvenile delinquency
- Revocation of conditional release
- Criminal versatility

If you find yourself identifying with all of the above traits, I suggest running to the nearest psychiatrist you can find!

I found the book fascinating!

FINDING JOBS THAT FIT YOUR DREAM JOB CHARACTERISTICS

Once you have found those characteristics (hopefully not from the PCL-R test) that bring you happiness and motivation, you can further explore what potential jobs might match those characteristics. One way to do that is to Google your traits and see what results:

Sample searches:
- Jobs that require travel
- Jobs in leadership
- Flex time jobs
- Jobs in sales
- Jobs that require critical analysis
- Creative jobs
- High paying jobs
- Jobs for extroverts
- Jobs for introverts
- Creating my own job description
- Jobs that require using my hands
- Outdoor only jobs
- Jobs for computer programmers
- Jobs in healthcare
- Jobs in fashion design
- Jobs involving persuasion
- Jobs where I can speak in front of a crowd
- Jobs with little writing requirements
- Jobs that require math; don't require math
- Jobs focused on food

YOUR DREAM JOB TITLE

Another way to find job titles that might fit your dream job position is to scour the job boards for titles and job descriptions that match what you are interested in (based on the aforementioned process). For example, in the sample search about food jobs, you can click on any of the links and obtain descriptions of available jobs that meet the qualities you wish for in your dream job.

In the next chapter, the section on JOB BOARDS will give you a more detailed description of industry specific job boards that you can search and that might fit your interests. I recommend initially spending time on the larger job boards such as Monster or Career Builder to obtain sample titles of potentially interesting jobs. However, I do not recommend applying to them yet.

Once you have an idea of potential job titles, you can further explore specialized job boards in those particular industries. I have found that the leading specialized job boards in each industry can be deeper and most relevant.

Do not forget to search on INDEED.COM as well as this is an aggregated search site of all jobs available, including those on company websites that may not be posted on job boards.

Make a list of the traits/categories that make you happy and start to fill in the jobs accordingly.

Two Review

!

(i) Take time to dream about what makes you happy

(i) Answer the self assessment questions

(i) Take career and personality test(s)

(i) Search job titles based on characteristics

(i) Search job boards for potential job titles and descriptions that interest you

(i) Make a list of job titles that most interest you

(i) Make sure you do not pass the psychopath test

THREE - HOW TO FIND YOUR
DREAM JOB

!

I have a client firm that uses an online screening tool for résumés. I am not a big believer in this methodology. Not only because I do personal in depth screening and matching for a living, but for the fact that a piece of paper does not the individual make.

Companies look for a particular background, accomplishment or schooling before they will even consider a candidate. If they only screen via a quantum algorithm, I believe they are missing the giant sequoia in the middle of the forest. Regardless, technology does have its value and in this particular case, the firm valued it very much. At the same time, they asked me to help them find the right candidate for a particular mid level role.

I contacted job seekers that I believed had the right background and proceeded to screen them deeper than the paper they provided. I narrowed down my list and recommended 4 candidates for the role. I gave a detailed overview of each job seeker, included their personal goals and career aspirations, as well as their perspective on the firm and how they specifically saw themselves adding value to the organization. It just so happened that one of the candidates had loaded his résumé onto the particular screening technology site in the hopes of being found. He was.

The Human Resources Manager at the firm explained to me that they had found this particular candidate's résumé via a parsing algorithm, and that they had already passed on him. I was shocked. This candidate was perfect for the role. I knew this because I knew the head of the company, what his goals were for the division and exactly the type of person he wanted to bring on. This particular job seeker was exactly what he asked for. However, on paper this candidate didn't fit boxes 4 and 5, so he was a 'pass.' To make matters worse for the candidate, not only did he have no idea that he was being considered for the role, but he was not aware that the company had passed over him. Now how can someone follow up on a potential opportunity when he is operating in the ether?

I recommended that the job seeker drop the technology platform, primarily because the platform had not alerted him to the fact that he had been matched to a particular job and was passed over. To make matters worse, he was paying for this service! This service was operating under their own exclusive banner of *don't ask - don't tell*. The candidate dropped the service and I had him placed at an excellent firm within a month.

I am not saying that a Recruiter is your only option, yet I am saying be careful as to which technology platforms or job boards you choose to upload your résumé to. You do not want to be everywhere, yet you do want to be where you will gain the most traction.

JOB BOARDS

There are many job boards where you can look for actual open positions that match your skill set, background and dream job aspirations. You should search them to see what type of job is a fit for you, yet I do not recommend loading your résumé onto every job board out there as this will water down your desirability.

As you find actual positions on job boards, create a tab on your Spread Sheet for the hiring company and cut and paste the job description onto the page.

Do not rush to send your C.V. as you need to do your homework on the company, the contact you will want to reach out to and how your cover letter and résumé may need to be crafted to fit the position (if, in fact, this is the ideal role for you). Maybe it is not, yet you now know that the company is hiring. Put a (*) next to the company name in the tab so that you know that particular company is hiring.

Again, I do not recommend jumping the gun and applying or loading your résumé onto a job board database. I want your first shot to be your best shot. I do not want you to get passed over because you do not fit into a checklist at an initial screening. I want you to get the interview the first time around!

The job board search should be simply to find your dream job or dream company. If you happen to find the dream position, that's even better.

Here is a listing of some job boards that can be helpful depending on what stage you are in with your job search.

Spend a day looking. Fill out your spread sheet and get motivated that you have lots of companies to approach!

GENERAL JOB BOARDS
www.watchthatpage.com (you can track jobs on particular company websites)
www.simplyhired.com (combs all posted jobs and jobs on company sites)
www.indeed.com (combs all posted jobs)
www.linkup.com
www.usjobs.com
www.monster.com
www.linkedin.com (top recommendation)
www.careerbuilder.com
www.jobfox.com

www.beyond.com
www.snagajob.com
www.job.com

NICHE JOB BOARDS

ACCOUNTING/FINANCIAL/BANKING

www.accountingjobstoday.com
www.accounting.com
www.jobsinthemoney.com
www.efinancialcareers.com
www.fins.com
www.onewire.com
www.theladders.com
www.bankjobs.com
www.careerbank.com
www.vault.com
www.accountingboard.com
www.financeitjobs.com
www.ihireaccounting.com
www.wallstreetoasis.com/finance-jobs

FASHION

www.stylecareers.com (fashion designers post here)
www.fiber2fashion.com
http://www.fashion.net/jobs

CULINARY

http://www.starchefsjobfinder.com
http://www.chef2chef.net/indeed/
http://culinary.imodules.com/s/898/cs.aspx?sid=898
&gid=1&pgid=264

PART TIME JOBS

www.momcorps.com
http://www.snagajob.com/part-time-jobs/
http://jobs.monster.com/v-part-time.aspx

RENEWABLE ENERGY

http://cleantechjobs.cleantechies.com/a/jobs/find-jobs

RETAIL

http://www.allretailjobs.com/

WRITING & MEDIA JOBS

www.mediabistro.com
http://www.writejobs.com
http://www.mediajobs.net

EDUCATION

www.schoolspring.com
http://www.topschooljobs.org
http://www.nationjob.com/education

LAW ENFORCEMENT

www.lawenforcementjobs.com
http://www.golawenforcement.com/jobs.htm
http://www.officer.com/careers

CONSTRUCTION

www.constructionjobs.com
http://www.careerbuilder.com/Jobs/Industry/Construction/

ENERGY

http://www.professionalenergyjobs.com
http://www.energyjobs.com

ENGINEERING

http://www.engineerjobs.com/

HEALTHCARE

http://www.healthcarejobs.org
http://www.healthcarejobs.net

TECHNOLOGY

www.dice.com
http://www.simplyhired.com/a/jobs/list/q-technology

ALL OTHER

http://www.jobboardreviews.com
(This site lists a plethora of niche job boards in every industry depending on your interest. Too many to name)

ADDITIONAL NICHE JOB BOARDS
http://www.internetinc.com

- accounting
- construction
- cruise ship
- data entry
- engineering
- college
- environmental
- finance
- freelance
- government
- graphic design
- healthcare
- hospitality
- insurance
- it
- journalism
- law enforcement
- marketing
- medical
- nursing
- overseas
- part time
- police
- retail
- sales
- security
- teaching
- warehouse
- welding
- work from home

CORPORATE WEBSITES

You can peruse company websites according to your target list of companies or do searches on the aggregate search engines that will bring up company names that are hiring. As you visit each company website, you can apply directly to those positions that fit your background and interests. I recommend, however, finding out the name of the person in charge of the department that is listing the position and communicating with him or her directly first, before submitting your C.V.

Remember also to conduct a search on Hoovers, Google and/or ZoomInfo to find out the competitors to a particular company. Visit their websites as well.

If you find an exact match on a company website that you are interested in and you simply are too worried that if you don't apply right now then someone else may get the position, then you may want to submit your credentials to the company website. However, if you do so, be sure to follow up with the person in charge of that division.

REFERRALS

Quite simply, ask. Ask your colleagues, ask people you have met in your industry, ask your social media connections and ask executives you have met at conferences or trade shows. Don't hound or stalk; yet it is OK to ask if a particular contact can refer you to a certain company that they know or work at. It is acceptable to ask a relationship if they can recommend someone for you to speak with at a company that they may know in the area of interest to you. Ask once, do not hound, do not stalk and always say thank you, regardless of the result.

Again, always say thank you!

GOLD MINE: THE HIDDEN JOBS

Did you know that hundreds of thousands of available jobs are not ever advertised? The primary reasons for this are:

- Companies do not want the competition finding out

- Companies are not perfectly sure of the actual title, yet they know in theory what they want.

- Companies do not want to deal with hundreds of résumés all at once.

One way that you can find some of these hidden jobs is by searching company career websites. Even though the positions may not be advertised, they are often posted on the company website.

You can also conduct searches for recruiters in the industry you are targeting. Many recruiting firms list their open positions. You can then contact the firm directly regarding their listing.

Many job boards will send you alerts when positions are posted that match your interests. Be selective, as you do not want your résumé to appear everywhere. People want what they can't have, not what they find open and available at every click of the mouse.

One such service that might interest you and from which you can receive job alerts is:

http://www.hound.com

The reason I like this service is that it sources from company websites as opposed to only scouring job boards.

Did you know that only about 5% of job seekers actually get jobs through job advertisements?

Many companies do not advertise their job openings beyond their own websites, so using a service like Hound could be advantageous. If you do decide to use such a service, or the alert service from targeted job boards (free or subscription based), I emphasize initially reaching out to the person in charge of the division that is hiring and mentioning that you saw the opening. Often times it is the HR department that receives your résumé via the website form and it is often that department that accepts or rejects you. I can tell you from experience that you will have more success going directly to the head of the department or the head of the firm. If that person refers you to HR, then that is fine, respect their process, as the referral comes from within which is valuable to you because you will put yourself at the front of the line.

Three Review

!

☉ Search aggregator job sites for job leads

☉ Search specialized job boards in your industry

☉ Upload your résumé to one or two niche job boards only

☉ Use subscription job boards sparingly

Now that you have determined what your dream job is, and have explored ways to find the actual job; let's learn the Hired! Secrets that will show you how to get to where you want to go.

FOUR – GET ORGANIZED

!

"Out of clutter, find simplicity" - *Albert Einstein*

Organization is crucial to your success in landing your next job, regardless if it is a lateral move, a move up the ladder or a job in a completely new field.

Maybe you scribble notes on pieces of paper, use an ipad for note taking and then email it to yourself or record your to-do list on your smartphone voice recorder. In my opinion, a lot depends on how you visualize your workflow.

As an Executive Recruiter, when I am on the telephone with the head of a company, I must be prepared. I must have detailed information, history of communication and my own perspective on the tip of my tongue or I will not transfer my knowledge seamlessly. Companies and job seekers come to me for my understanding, market knowledge, connections, perspective, and persuasive capabilities. I must be on top of everything - all at once.

I stay organized with an interconnected system that I believe can help you.

You may think that I subscribe to all of the fancy ATS (Applicant Tracking Systems) and sourcing software available, and believe me there are more than I wish to count. I trialled several of them, yet found myself spending more time inputting and searching for information as opposed to actually using the systems. The *search all* buttons never gave me what I wanted. I was not being productive and frankly, I was frustrated.

Out of frustration, I came up with an interlinking system that keeps me organized to this day beyond my own expectations. I am never at a loss when I am sitting at my desk and on the phone with an employer or candidate. I have everything I need at my fingertips. I am able to respond to questions and provide in depth information and perspective that adds value to the conversation beyond discussing someone's résumé. My revenues went up 100% a year after implementing this system.

I think this system will work for you and because I want you to have every advantage imaginable in your quest for that new position, I will explain it to you in detail.

S.P.E.E.D.

I call my organization system S.P.E.E.D. No, it has nothing to do with drugs, although the productivity realized when engaging this system can prove addictive.

I believe that by using this system, you will become so organized and have so much information at your fingertips, that you will S.P.E.E.D. up your search process and jump ahead of your competition in competing for that coveted position.

"S" IS FOR SPREAD SHEET

The "S" in S.P.E.E.D. stands for SPREAD SHEET.

What goes into the spread sheet?
In one word – everything! In terms of which format to use, I recommend using the program Excel, which is the most widely used spread sheet program on the market.

The value of a spread sheet system is that you can work from each page according to each company that you are targeting. With the S.P.E.E.D. method, you will be able to access everything you need to know about a particular company on one page, making it easier to see the whole picture of your process. It is also beneficial because you are not only able to search the existing page, but also the entire document with a click of the mouse.

Your starting point is to label the tabs at the bottom of the page with each company name that you are targeting.

There are four useful tools that you can use to create your list of 50-100 target companies.

www.google.com

www.zoominfo.com

www.hoovers.com

Job Boards

Perform searches on any of these sites based on key words such as the industry you are interested in and the location you prefer within that industry. You can also search competitors for each company that meets your criteria. Soon you will have a list of target companies that appeal to you. Add a tab for the companies you already wish to work for as well.

Job boards are not only for job titles, but also for the companies who are advertising their jobs. Add these companies to your tabs with an (*) as part of the tab name for the companies that are hiring presently.

In organizing your spread sheet, I recommend columns that include company name, contact information and action steps. You can make as many columns as you need based on how much information you wish to include. With this method, you can also print out all of the relevant information on one page to take with you and prep from while you are waiting for your interview. I recommend setting up the page in landscape format so that you have room for more columns.

Here is an example of the starting point for a company page.

	A	B	C	D	E	F	G	H	I
1	Company	Address	City	State	Zip	Phone	Contact	Title	Email
4	Clothing to Go	908 Montgomery St.	SF	CA	94111	(800) 888-1050	Sue Jones	Head of HR	sjones@gallery.com
5									
6	Inquiry	Response	Next Steps	Interview	Follow Up				
7	tel: 1/22/2012	interested	tel 1/28	1-Feb					
8				2pm					
9	NOTES								
10	Spoke with Sue on 1/28 for 25 min. Discussed my background. She is from NJ originally like me. Went over my background and my								
11	suggestions for a new urban belt line that I discovered when I was visiting my cousin in New Orleans. She asked me to come in to meet								
12	the team and could I bring pictures/samples of the belt line? She has 2 young kids. Talked about how hard the retail market is now.								
13	Remember to do market analysis on growth trends and bring that with me to interview. Address retail outlook forecast.								
14									
15									
16									
17									
18									

As you can see, everything I need to know about my communication with Company A so far is on one page and in one document. You can cut and paste your email communications and put them on this page as well.

You can also highlight certain action steps to make sure that you do not miss them, (such as when your interview is scheduled!).

The key to using a spread sheet is to have everything on ONE SPREAD SHEET. That's right, you do not want to have to open a zillion spread sheets for each job search you conduct. You can work from one for everything. Keep it simple and you will use it every day.

I create one spread sheet for each year of recruiting. It is massive but I have access to everything at all times with the touch of a touchpad.

The benefit of having one spread sheet is three fold:

- Simplicity so that you do not get overwhelmed.

- Capability to add as many tabs as you need – on one document.

- Ability to search the page or the entire spread sheet with just one click.

It would also be wise to add a column with your company contact's background information. Look them up on the corporation's website, review their LinkedIn profile for their work history and note any potential pieces of information that you might have in common. Also be sure to conduct a search of that person on Google. You might learn that they have written an article, have been quoted in the press or serve on a board. Do your research and include the essentials for each company page on your spread sheet.

SCHEDULE YOUR SPREAD SHEET

As you make progress with each company, I recommend scheduling follow-ups, phone calls and meetings onto your spread sheet as well as into your handheld device calendar or reminder program right away. I input follow-ups with the company name, contact and agenda. For meetings, I enter date, time, location, contact. I often add a short note in the notes section of the appointment that highlights what I plan to discuss or achieve at the meeting or on the scheduled phone call.

I also highly recommend assigning a reminder 30 minutes in advance for a phone call and 2 hours in advance for a meeting. That way you will have time to reflect prior to the phone call (and get there in time if it is an in-person interview!).

PERSONAL NETWORK

In addition to the Company Tabs, you should have a tab that says Network. This is the page where you input all of your personal contacts with whom you would like to connect and that you think can help you. This is different from contacts you may have on LinkedIn, Google+, Facebook, Twitter or other Social/Business media.

Here is an example of how your Personal Network page may appear.

	C	D	E	F	G	H
1	Name	Phone	Title	Email	Relationship	Contacted
2	Bob Jones	415-891-7786	Ex-Pres of Urban Clothes	bjones@gmail.com	Tennis friend	Tel/1-19
3						
4	Notes					
5	Spoke with Bob on the phone about my desire to join a retail clothing company. Worked in clothing					
6	merchandising but my company went 100% ecommerce and eliminated my clothing buyer role. He told me					
7	about a new company that a friend of his was launching that focuses on board shorts for women. Said to use					
8	his name. Sarah Billings/Bored Shorts. They are online and have one retail store in SF.					
9	sbillings@boredshorts.com.					
10	Follow Up					
11	thanks to Bob 1/19					
12	contact him after connecting with Sarah					
13						
14	Name	Phone	Title	Email	Relationship	Contacted
15	Karen Foust	415-888-6234	VP Merchandising/Gap	kfoust@yahoo.com	School Mom	vm 2/1
16						
17	Notes					
23						
24						
25						
26	Follow Up					
27	em on 2/3					
28						
29						
30						

NAME   PHONE   TITLE

Bob Jones   415-891-7786   Ex-Pres of Urban Clothes

EMAIL   RELATIONSHIP   CONTACTED

bjones@gmail.com   Tennis Friend   Tel/1-19

NOTES

Spoke with Bob on phone about my desire to join a retail clothing company. Worked in clothing merchandising but my company went 100% ecommerce and eliminated my clothing buyer role. He told me about a new company that a friend of his was launching that focuses on board shorts for women. Said to use his name. Sarah Billings/Bored shorts. They are online and have one retail store in SF. sbillings@boredshorts.com

FOLLOW UP

Thanks to Bob 1/19. Contact him after connecting with Sarah.

NAME   PHONE   TITLE

Karen Foust   415-888-6234   VP Merchandising/Gap

EMAIL   RELATIONSHIP   CONTACTED

kfoust@yahoo.com   School Mom   vm 2/1

NOTES

As you connect with your personal network and discover new opportunities (such as Bob Jones's friend who runs Bored Shorts), you will, of course, make a new Company Tab to add Bored Shorts to the opportunity mix.

COVER LETTER AND C.V. TABS

You should also add a tab for your general cover letter and your résumé so that you have quick access at the click of a mouse. C.V. means Curriculum Vitae, and is another word for résumé. I suggest using it.

On the cover letter tab you can simply cut and paste your general cover letter. Feel free to paste several types of cover letters based on the type of company you are targeting.

EXAMPLE

Dear Ms. Jones,

I am a 10+ year merchandising manager for a leading clothing line owned by Urbane Clothiers. You may have heard that Urbane has decided to convert to a 100% Ecommerce model. As a result, I am currently exploring new opportunities in clothing merchandising. I am familiar with Clothing To Go and am particularly impressed with how the company has moved into the city dweller market with its new line of muted tones and edgy accessories. I came across several of your designs during my tenure at Urbane.

I would love to buy you a cup of coffee in the next week or so to learn more about your expansion plans. In particular, I have discovered a new belt line that I think could be an ideal product for Clothing To Go. I am in personal discussions with the creator to distribute the line.

Ideally, I am seeking to join a company where I can be part of a visionary team that wants to be a leader in the clothing and accessory market, both online and in retail stores.

I look forward to hearing back from you and to meeting with you as your near term schedule allows.

Sincerely,

You

If you customize your cover letter for each company, you can add it to the appropriate company page as well.

Please note that, for spread sheet purposes, you should change the actual formatting for the cover letter so that it fits onto the spread sheet.

Note: If you cut and paste your cover letter onto one line in your spread sheet, it will stay on that line and continue out to the right for too many pages and you will not be able to see it unless you click on the line. It will not print out on a single page.

Note: Refer to the chapter on Cover Letters for structural direction when it comes to actually writing and sending your cover letter.

If you already have a job description that you have found and are applying to at a particular company, add a column for that as well.

I think you are getting the idea, which is to have as much of your detailed information as possible in one place in a condensed, easy referenced format. Use abbreviations if you need to. Make it simple and clear with essential information only.

On the C.V. Tab, you can cut and paste your C.V. so that you have it accessible on your spread sheet. You can also open the PDF file of your actual C.V. (I recommend keeping it on your computer desktop file in a .doc or .docx format *and* PDF format) and tile the windows side by side so that you can refer to it at the same time if you do not wish to toggle to it during a phone interview. This is what I do when I am on the phone with a company client. I open my spread sheet and the candidate's CV at the same time. Because I deal with tens of thousands of candidates, I cannot put every C.V. on my single spread sheet. I do, however, cut and paste the candidate's C.V.'s onto the company client tab where I have submitted them for consideration. This way I have all relevant information on one screen. I usually pair down the C.V. to the essentials so that I can see everything on one page.

"P" IS FOR PAPER

The "P" in S.P.E.E.D. is for PAPER.

It's not that I am old fashioned, but studies have shown that the eye remembers many more details when they are written by hand. The science goes on to say that by writing things down, we are putting more thought into the process and are subconsciously filtering out unimportant information while keeping core information in order. This helps to keep the details in our brains - even more so that typing.

I have read many articles and studies that discuss how the hand-brain connection works. Google *writing by hand helps us remember*, and decide for yourself.

When I am on the telephone with candidates or companies, I take notes. Well, actually it looks more like scribble sometimes. I write things down in a spiral notebook and use a separate notebook for each month of the year. Why do I do this? Four reasons.

- I want to make sure that I don't miss anything during the conversation

- I write my personal impressions in the notebook as they occur to me

- I always remember the exact conversation when I look back at my notes (especially based on HOW I wrote down the information)

- I space my notebooks out so that I can refer to them easily

  ○ I talk to a lot of people in any given month

  ○ You may only need one notebook for your entire job search

Immediately after I get off of the telephone or out of a meeting, I highlight certain elements in my notes such as date, name, title, impression, companies I am thinking of sending a candidate to or type of candidate I understand that the company wants (if it is a conversation with a client company). I then type a more detailed account of the conversation (taking care to include the highlighted elements) into my spread sheet. It's akin to a double opt-in formula where someone signs up for something with an email and then they get an email saying 'are you sure?' which they have to reply back to, essentially saying 'sure, I'm sure.'

When you are on the telephone with a network contact, a hiring manager, an administrative assistant, or whoever it is in relation to your job search, you should take notes long hand first.

Use a spiral NOTEBOOK. Do not compile notes on napkins, post-its, or the back of your hand. Open a fresh new page of your spiral notebook for every conversation.

Start by putting the date in the upper left or right hand corner. Put the date in the same place on every page.

I can't tell you how many times I have referred to my spread sheets from years past and wanted to remember the 'feel' of a particular conversation as well. I simply went back to the corresponding date in the correct notebook, flipped to the page I needed and voila, I remembered the tone of the conversation and all of my impressions. I remembered the conversation as though it had happened that same day, not only by what I had written, but how I wrote it. Sometimes I wrote words with heavy underlining, large circles around phrases or exclamation points. "Personable "Grew up in NJ like me," "Funny!" "Pushy," "Arrogant," "Messy Divorce," etc.

Write down what the person on the other end of the phone is saying. Write single words or short phrases describing your impression, an idea that strikes you, a particular follow up you want to make. And then transpose the information onto your spread sheet, which is what you will refer to most of the time.

When you need to go back in time to a particular conversation in your notebook, you will be amazed at the details you remember, almost down to the sound of the person's voice.

SUMMARY

- Create a "S" Spread sheet with tabs for:

  - Each Target Company

  - Personal Network

  - Cover letter

  - CV/Résumé

When on the phone, take longhand notes. After an in-person interview, take longhand notes and then transpose all notes onto your spread sheet.

Along with the "S" in SPREADSHEET, the other program I have open at all times is:

"E" IS FOR EMAIL

The "E" in S.P.E.E.D. is for Email

I never delete my business emails. Ever. Why? Because I need to keep track of every communication that I have with a person. Of course, I also cut and paste many of these emails into my spread sheet.

I used to use Entourage, yet when I switched to Apple, I switched to Mac Mail. In the search bar at the top, I enter a person's name and then click the 'from' sorting category at the top of the email string. This puts all of the emails with that person in order. I do not always cut and paste every email into my spread sheet (only the action step emails) as I communicate with so many candidates it would not make sense. I do put all of my client emails in my spread sheet so that I have them in one place. Your process will be more akin to my dealing with clients, so I suggest that you do cut and paste your email communications into your spread sheet. However, it is up to you. Your checkpoint should be such that you are able to see all relevant information on your spread sheet on one page. Use common sense. Don't include the emails that say 'thanks,' 'looking forward to it,' and simple gestures as such, but do include the informative and action oriented email exchanges. My focus is in keeping my spread sheet condensed and concise so that I can see the entire page at once and can inspect all pertinent information (even if abbreviated) in a single view.

My goal is to have little to no scrolling. I can adjust the columns so that they are narrower, decrease the font size and highlight with colored fill, certain elements that are important as it relates to that particular person or client. It is a matter of preference. Do what feels comfortable and is ease of use for you.

When I am on the phone with a company or candidate, I pull up my spread sheet and my email (and the CV if it is a candidate) and I am fully prepared.

The goal is to keep your information together for easy access.

"E" IS FOR EDUCATE

Being organized includes keeping yourself informed and educated about the companies that you are communicating with. You should have a column on your spread sheet that gives an overview of the company, its strengths, competitors, information about the person you are interviewing with and a column as to how you add value. You will be amazed at how helpful this will be for you when you are on the telephone with a prospective employer.

You can list these columns under the contact display.

Example: Choices of Tabs and Categories

	B	C	D	E	F	G	H	I	J	K
1 Company	Address	City	State	Zip	Phone	Contact	Title	Email		
2										
3										
4 Inquiry	Response	Next Steps	Interview	Follow Up						
5										
6										
7										
8										
9 Overview	Strengths/Weakneses	Competitors	About JOE SMITH		HOW I ADD VALUE					
10										
11										
12 Notes										
13										
14										
15										
16										
17 EMAILS										
18										
19										
20										
21										

COMPANY

ADDRESS   CITY   STATE   ZIP

PHONE   CONTACT   TITLE   EMAIL

INQUIRY   RESPONSE   NEXT STEPS

INTERVIEW   FOLLOW UP

OVERVIEW   STRENGTHS   WEAKNESSES

COMPETITORS   ABOUT CONTACT   HOW I ADD VALUE

We all get nervous which is why you will want to have as much relevant information at your fingertips as possible. The last thing you will want to do is spend your time tiling between windows of information or racking your brain for ideas when you are on the phone with a prospective employer.

When I have status calls with clients, I open up my spread sheet, which contains all of the pertinent information about our communications, information about my client, the candidates I have recommended and what I want to achieve during that particular call. I have everything at my fingertips. I am informed and ready to field any and all questions. You will benefit from having all pertinent information in front of you.

NOTE: If you assign one company per page of your spread sheet, you should have plenty of room. Widen or narrow the columns to fit in the email strings, the information about the firm, the person's title and background who is interviewing you, and all other information discussed - all on one sheet for quick reference.

"D" IS FOR DETAILS

It's all in the details. If you are good at keeping track of details, you will be good at organization. If you are conducting more than 25 job searches, one way to keep track of your job searches and applications, for example, is to use a site like http://www.huntsy.com, which enables you to keep track of the many job searches you explore in your quest. It keeps the details organized as you apply to each job and reminds you what you need to do next for a particular position. Think of it as your personal application tracking system. Although it may not be as useful if you are simply contacting someone at a particular company that may not be advertising a position.

While using a job search program might fit your work style better, I still recommend cutting and pasting your progress into your spread sheet so that you have everything in one place and on one page as you prepare for your interviews.

I am not a big fan of tiling between several information sources. I like everything on one page in front of me. Maybe this is because I speak and meet with at least 50 people a week. You may be different. Choose what works best for you.

As you move forward with your job pursuit, you will also want to keep your desktop calendar updated with follow up reminders, appointments and notes to yourself. If you are on a cloud system, when you add a reminder or appointment on your mobile phone, it will appear on your desktop or laptop calendar as well. I schedule everything, including putting a note on my spread sheet, that I am following up on X date. Again, everything on one page, but use all of the tools you need to aggregate the details and keep yourself organized. The best part? When you refer back to your one page spread sheet, you will have all of your progress right in front of you without toggling between pages or icons on a tracking system.

I also do not like to be at the whim of an online system that I may not have access to at all times. My spread sheet is on my desktop and laptop. I can email it to my smartphone or print it out and take it with me. I feel more in control than relying on a network program. I also don't like to upload all of my trustworthy client and candidate information onto an external company system. I deal in confidentiality, so I tend to keep things close.

You may be different. You may enjoy the bells and whistles of an online system. I tend to lean toward simplicity and core information.

I also love the fact that I can go back to my yearly spread sheets and notebooks and have everything related to one transaction (including all of my idiosyncratic impressions) on one page, forever.

ROUTINE

Finally, you will S.P.E.E.D. up your success if you make a definite decision to implement a pattern of behaviour; a daily routine that you can rely on to keep yourself organized and current each day.

This routine should dovetail with your style and undulating biorhythms. It should be comfortable enough to become a habit. Finding your dream job will take dedication and persistence. If you have a routine that you can rely on, the process will fly by and soon you will be sitting in the seat of your ideal profession.

I am a morning person. I like to get up early, read my emails on my smartphone and read three newspapers. I have a cup of decaf coffee during this routine. I used to drink caffeinated coffee, but it made my heart race, so I enjoy the same warmth and taste with decaf. I also find that I remain focused and not jittery when I drink decaf as opposed to caffeinated drinks.

After I 'catch up,' (which makes me feel successful before I even get out of bed!) I put on my running clothes and go for a jog. I do most of my creative thinking during my runs. I craft my plans for the day, set short and long term goals and resolve issues.

After exercising, I get something to eat, take a quick shower and head into the office. I am already ahead of the game. My endorphins have kicked in, I am in front of the communication curve and I am shifting into accomplishment mode. If you are a morning person, I suggest starting your day with some form of exercise. It will wake you up, energize you and clear your mind to start the day - fresh and ready for success.

Much of my day revolves around many little steps and activities that drive me closer to my weekly or monthly goal.

I do find that I am more productive during certain hours of the day, so often around 1 or 2, I take a break. My mind needs a rest. I go for a walk outside, close my eyes for 10 minutes or wander around the Internet looking at funny videos, messages from friends on Facebook or I play with my puppy (that is if I work from home that day). Then it's back to work. Right before I leave the office, I leave several voicemails for people I have been trying to reach and seek to set up a time to connect over the next couple of days.

As evening approaches, I make a nice dinner, visit with my family and relax. Once the house is quiet, I usually open up my laptop and work on one of my creative projects. This is my reward for a hard day of work and I always look forward to it. I get so involved that sometimes I lose track of time.

Right before I close down for the night, I send a few emails with the intention of receiving a reply the following day. It is a great way to end the day and it gives me positive anticipation for the next morning.

Determine when you are the most productive and schedule your intense job seeking tasks (including interviews) during the time when you are most alert and at peak form.

Give yourself a break during the day - several if needed.

You will want to keep yourself motivated, so make sure that you schedule some fun time for yourself every day. Maybe that is a walk, bike ride or a quick game of tennis. Do what makes you happy; just make sure it is something physical that will awaken your brain cells.

I also suggest scheduling a short block of time to indulge in a creative activity each day. Read a chapter of a book or peruse a magazine; draw a picture or play a game of *Words With Friends*. It helps your productivity output to get out of your work mentality and let the other side of your brain have some fun. Do something that is emotionally pleasing.

SECRET: Our best ideas and decisions come to us when we are aligned with our most positive emotional state. Seek to find that state at some point every day.

Four Review

!

- ⓘ *S* IS FOR SPREADSHEET

- ⓘ *P* IS FOR PAPER

- ⓘ *E* IS FOR EMAIL

- ⓘ *E* IS FOR EDUCATION

- ⓘ *D* IS FOR DETAILS

Five - What Kind Of A Job Seeker Are You?

!

I was FIRED!

Really?

Is that how you refer to yourself? Maybe you were let go, laid off, terminated, RIF'd, downsized, were part of a reorganization or are working out your exit package.

Lesson One: There are many ways to say you were fired without saying

I WAS FIRED!

- Let go

- Part of a reorganization

- Position was eliminated

- Laid off

- RIF'd (reduction in force)

- Downsized

- Working out an exit package

- Parted Ways

- Mutual Agreement

- Terminated

- Part of the economic downturn

- Outsourced

- Role was brought in-house

- On the Beach

- Displaced

- Not a great fit

- Part of the merger

- New management brought in their own people

Regardless of the circumstances that may have led to your current 'in transition' status, you are in need of a job. In Recruiter lingo, you are considered an ACTIVE candidate because you are actively in the job market. This book was written for you.

!

Are you currently gainfully employed, yet have an eye out for something better? Maybe the *better* consists of a lateral move that pays more or enables you to join a company higher up the pecking order in your industry. Maybe you are thinking of a complete career change.

Regardless of your reason for opening your mind to new opportunities, if you are currently employed, you are considered a PASSIVE candidate and this book was written for you.

Does the word 'candidate' bother you? Do you feel like less than a number or piece of paper on a stack that is on its way to the recycling bin? Do you feel like an email relegated to the spam folder?

Sorry to break it to you, but this is how you are referred. Embrace your status because now you are 'in the know' and have a glimpse into what it looks like for you at the starting line.

You may be wondering – is it better to be an ACTIVE or PASSIVE candidate?

Let me break it to you gently.

It is better to be a PASSIVE candidate.

Why? Because just like the restaurant that takes six months to get into (i.e. The French Laundry in Napa, California), people want what others want and what they can't have right now. If you are immediately available (other than within the last few weeks), you are not initially as attractive to employers. In HIRED! I will show you how to make yourself just as desirable as the passive candidate.

If you are a passive candidate, you may be sitting their confidently thinking, *Hey, I'm in the driver's seat.*

Yes, you are by virtue of the fact that you are likely collecting a paycheck, are not desperate and can hopefully take your time looking for the next key move in your career.

However, you are not really in the driver's seat if where you are now is not where you want to be.

If you are seeking an entirely new career direction, you are on par with the Active Candidates. For example, if you want to work at a bigger, better firm, you will have to do some good selling to be considered. If you want to downsize and become a big fish in a small pond (a very noble move in many industries), then yes, in that case, you are more in the driver's seat. However, you might be too big for that little fish pond and may scare the minnows away.

Not to worry. Wherever you are in your process, I will give you the guidance, the inside scoop and the information you need to know to get where you want to go as quickly as possible.

For all of you Active Candidates who are out of work and looking for your dream job, do not be discouraged! One of your great advantages is that you can start work today! Starting right away can be very attractive to the right company at the right time. We will talk about how to prepare yourself for that position and how to put your absolute best foot forward in securing your dream job, just like your passive counterpart.

Note: I must tell you that I am not a licensed psychiatrist or psychologist or lawyer. But I am a very successful Recruiter, which means, in part, that I am a very good listener - and I have learned a lot through that key skill. If there is one sneak preview of advice that I can give you as you seek the next rewarding step up your occupational ladder – LISTEN! More than any other skill, you will find the most value in mastering the art of listening.

I have listened to CEOs, Heads of Human Resources, Middle Managers, Account Executives (that means sales people), Admin (administrative roles such as assistant to the head honcho), top producers who have titles like Managing Director and Partner, Passive Candidates, Active Candidates and my own internal voice. It all adds up to being able to help many wonderful people like you land excellent jobs.

Now you might be saying, *Yeah, but you only fill jobs on Wall Street. How can you help someone who is in IT or telemarketing or roofing or healthcare or retail?*

You would be amazed at how people are similar across any and all disciplines. The Head of Asset Management at a bulge bracket firm has kids that play soccer or basketball or baseball. They want the coach to play their kid. The coach might only make $10 an hour, but that executive values the coach enormously. In this case, the coach is the hiring manager and the executive has to get the job for his kid. We are all job seekers and hiring managers at some point along our path, and we can learn valuable lessons from either perspective.

RELATIONSHIPS

Life is about relationships. Whether it's on the playing field, at home or in the office, you need to build relationships in order to culminate your efforts toward a successful outcome: a happy marriage, a well adjusted child, a job that fits. People are people no matter what industry they are in and regardless if you are interviewing to be the night shift security guard at your local shopping mall or the next CEO of Microsoft, you need to build successful relationships. How do you start to do that? By finding:

COMMON GROUND

Common Ground is the first step to developing any relationship and moving any opportunity forward. I am going to help you learn how to find it so that when you set out to land the interview for your dream job, you will know what to say and do to establish common ground and be on your way to getting that offer.

In summary, whether you are an Active or Passive job seeker, there are pluses and minuses to any situation. In HIRED!, we are going to bring out the positives of your personal situation and position you for that next move up your career ladder. You will learn how to network, develop common ground and build relationships in order to move your career forward toward the ultimate goal of securing your dream job!

Five Review

!

ⓘ Active Candidates are unemployed and initially, are less desirable to hire.

ⓘ Active Candidates are motivated and can start work tomorrow, which is a key advantage.

ⓘ Passive Candidates are employed, and in general, are more desirable to hire.

ⓘ Passive Candidates must look further into the future and risk a lost opportunity.

ⓘ If you are an Active Candidate, I will show you how to turn your status into passive.

ⓘ If you are a Passive Candidate, I will show you how to create urgency.

ⓘ We are all 'Candidates' in the eyes of the Employer.

ⓘ BUILDING RELATIONSHIPS IS A CORE
ELEMENT OF FINDING THE RIGHT
OPPORTUNITIES.

ⓘ FINDING COMMON GROUND IS STEP
ONE IN YOUR JOB QUEST

SIX - HOW ACTIVE CANDIDATES CAN APPEAR PASSIVE

!

I try not to *judge a book by its cover* or *expect the best and assume the worst.* I don't necessarily live by the belief that *a chain is only as strong as its weakest link.* After all, couldn't it also be said that *in our weakness thereby lies our greatest strength*?

On the other hand, I am also a realist. We live in a world where people like and often need to compartmentalize. Too often we reduce our lives to clichés, labels and epithets just in order to get through the myriad of demands on our attention.

In this world of technological advances and shrinking turn around time, our de facto fall back is to make judgments and assign labels. It is natural. Maybe it is not fair, but *it is what it is* and we all do it. The key is to embrace this behaviour and present yourself in such a way as to attract the lasting cliché or label that you desire. Be revered as the *ace in the hole* or the one who keeps his *nose to the grindstone.* Strive to be the one who has her *head in the game* and it just might be that *dancing to the beat of your own drummer* is what will make you *stand out from the crowd.*

As for your current label of *Active Job Seeker,* the reality is - you are out of work. Your bills are mounting and you are dipping into savings (if you have any at all). You may have been looking for work for a month or for more than a year. The bottom line - you need a job! And to make matters worse, the longer you are out of work, the harder it may be to re-enter the work force.

Psychologists have documented the decrease in self-esteem that occurs from being out of work, regardless of the reason. Unemployed people tend to feel that they are no longer valuable. People who are out of work face the cold hard reality that yes, they are replaceable. Some job seekers may even fall into depression and not know how to get out of the emotional jobless rut that they are in. This may be you.

Are you collecting unemployment? That too will end after 26 weeks. It can be a Catch 22. You can't find work and you are surviving on unemployment, but the longer you live off of unemployment, the harder it will be to find work. Viscous cycle!

In the eyes of the potential employer you are an ACTIVE Candidate. You are actively seeking employment. Unfortunately, this label is also code for *desperate, willing to take anything, bottom of the pile* or simply *unemployable*. Why should an employer take a chance on you?

The GOOD NEWS is that just because you are unemployed, it does not mean that you are unemployable. You still have the same great skills that you had in your last job and hopefully you are ready to put those skills back to work as soon as possible.

The GOOD NEWS is that there are ways for you to alter this biased perception, label or cliché and present yourself in such a way as to create interest from potential employers.

Let's put you on par with the PASSIVE candidate.

HOW DO YOU MAKE YOURSELF APPEAR PASSIVE WHEN YOU ARE ACTIVE? HERE'S HOW!

First, you create a position for yourself that embodies what you are doing while you are officially unemployed. I highly doubt that you are sitting around the house eating bonbons all day and watching TV in your pajamas. Wait! You are? Well that's just dandy, because you are not a loser, you are a Researcher and a Blogger! You are researching the effect of television watching on eating habits or the lack of exercise on depression and you are your own Guiney Pig. You are writing a daily blog about how you are gaining or losing weight and eating certain foods based on the shows you are watching.

Or maybe you are writing a blog about how you are hunting for a job. You can record yourself in front of your computer as you chronicle your job search efforts and post daily or weekly reports to YouTube. Just make sure to look sharp!

You may be taking an online course to better your skill set so that you are more desirable to employers. You are a student! All employers value education; you are simply making sure that you provide more value to your future employer.

If you are unemployed, stop right now and think about what you do every day. Create a job description that you can use to fill in the gap between now and the first day of your dream job. Moreover, if you already know what your dream job is, start to do something each day (along with your job prospecting) that gets you one step closer *to* your Dream Job.

For example: I always wanted to be a writer. When I was an Investment Banker, I spent free moments on airplanes or in bed at night writing poetry. I got so good at using small blocks of time that I was able to publish several poems in many anthems and even won several poetry awards. One of my favourite stories in verse can still be ordered. It is called The Perfect Gift: A Christmas Story, by JB Miller (http://www.amazon.com/The-Perfect-Gift-Christmas-ebook/dp/B006J8M5JQ/ref=sr_1_1?s=digital-text&ie=UTF8&qid=1347574767&sr=1-1&keywords=a+christmas+story%2C+jb+miller). It is a story about the gift of time and I have sold many copies.

I completed a similar creative project when I was a strategic consultant. I wrote a song about my challenged son, hired a singer and musician, spent all night in a recording studio with my team and produced the song. I then approached the CEO of one of the companies I was consulting for (who distributed digital music to every radio station in the country) and asked him to send my song to every radio station in exchange for a free day of consulting. *Christopher's Song* ended up on the radio and is still downloaded today at: http://www.songstall.com/Butterfly.

I have since written a novel, a volume of short stories, many articles and blogs, and now this book to help you land your Dream Job!

The point I am making is that even if you are out of work, you can start doing things that will bring you closer to your dream job today. In the process, you will be filling the break in time that you are unemployed by having a solid interest, skill and carefully crafted position that you can put on your résumé. There will be no gap in your employment!

Volunteering is a great way to fill the space *and* to explore job opportunities. If you have always wanted to be a veterinarian for example, volunteer at your local animal shelter. If you have considered starting a business, volunteer at the local S.C.O.R.E. in your community or the Chamber of Commerce. If you are looking for connections in your community, visit a Rotary Club meeting and network! Do you need to brush up on your business acumen? Take an Excel or Forecasting class at your local Community College. Have you always wanted to get in shape? Start now and document your progress. You are in training for a 10k, a marathon, a triathlon, a sailing race, a tough mudder competition, or whatever activity interests you.

As you develop as an individual, blog about it. How do you do it? Just go to WordPress.com and sign up for a blog for free. You can even submit your blogs, articles or stories to online magazines or ezines as a freelance writer. Here are a few sites that pay for your work:

Yahoo! Contributor Network (previously called Associated Content).

You can keep the rights to your articles and publish on other sites as well as the Yahoo! site. You are paid when people view your article (approximately $1.50 per thousand monthly views). They even have an Assignment Desk where you can browse for writing topics. Even if you are not a writer, just browsing the topics may spark your interest in doing something during the hours when you are not looking for a job that may help you in your next interview. You get paid via PayPal, so set up a PayPal account before you venture down this road.

Here are some examples of topics that you can write about, or areas of focus that may spark ideas toward your dream job, or simply categories to inspire you to pursue now that you have more free time.

Auto * Health * Home Improvement * Lifestyle
*News * Sports * Technology * Travel * Business
* Entertainment

Let's take my earlier example of the Restaurant
Manager who got fired. He has a son who is a
ranked golfer and who is vying for a college
scholarship. What does he do now? He coaches his
son and is an assistant coach to the local high school
girl's golf team! What element of coaching is
transferable to his next job interview?

Leadership

Making decisions

Encouragement and Motivation

Ability to give and take constructive criticism

Ability to communicate

Flexibility

My point is - do SOMETHING right now that can
help you fill in the unemployment aperture and for
which you are passionate so that you can be
enthusiastic and interesting during your next
interview! If you have already figured out what
your dream job is, then begin focusing your efforts
on those skills, volunteer opportunities or hobbies
that will point you in the direction of your dream
job.

If you don't yet know what your dream job is and
are happy obtaining a position related to what you

have always done (and are happy to continue doing, hence, maybe you are already in your dream field) then brush up on a skill, volunteer for an organization that is related to your current industry or jump right in and begin informational interviews with a handful of target companies where you would like to work.

I know a woman who has never worked. She married young, raised four children, got divorced and decided that it was time to go to work. We sat down to discuss what it was that she loved to do most.

"Well, I love to wear new clothes and do fun things." Digging deeper, I found that what she meant was shopping. So I went shopping with her and watched how she interacted personally with every salesperson, making the entire experience fun. She laughed a lot, tried on crazy outfits and usually walked out with something in a shiny new bag. She made everyone happy, including herself. After our excursion we sat down at a local restaurant and long and behold, she knew all of the waiters and waitresses in the entire establishment. "I come here every Wednesday for their soup special," she smiled. Each waiter made their way to our table (almost as if choreographed) to give my friend an update about their personal situation.

"My mother is doing better." "I found an apartment." "He asked me to marry him." I watched how my friend interacted with anyone and everyone and then I knew. Retail! She should work in retail helping people find the right outfit and making them feel good in the process. She agreed. We made a list of her favourite stores and she went in to talk to the manager at each one. Every single shop wanted to hire her! She chose a much-loved boutique and I am happy to report that she started her first ever job a month ago. I went in to see her last week and left there with my own shiny new bag filled with her store's wears. She is a very good salesperson! I wonder if you even considered her age. She is, in fact, 51 years old! So for those Boomers out there who don't think they can re-enter the workforce, my friend did it, having never worked before. You can too!

My friend (an Active Job Seeker) embraced the fact that she needed a job, zeroed in on what she loved and boldly went for it. Her love of shopping and interacting with others shone through and voila, she is actively employed now.

All of the ideas I have mentioned will help you move from Active Job Seeker status to Passive Job Seeker status. You are not out of work. You are exploring other options, interests and passions. It's all a matter of perception, most importantly your perception of yourself. Trust me when I tell you that you are unique and you are an expert at something (like my friend is at shopping and interacting with others). By filling your free time with activities that will help you get closer to your dream job, you will bring much more vitality to your next interview, not to mention the fact that you may end up with a job offer just by volunteering or following your passion.

Once you have decided what it is that you are currently doing and have created a title for yourself, update your profile on LinkedIn as soon as possible. If you do not yet have a profile, please craft one now. The chapter on social media will show you how to make an appealing Linked In profile. No longer will your current role have an end date on it. Your new title is today's date until present, which means you are working!

Here are some sample titles that you can use for your current position that may help spark your thought process:

Assistant

Associate

Blogger

Caretaker

Coach

Consultant

Coordinator

Developer

Educator

Facilitator

Instructor

Liaison

Manager (of your house!)

Planner

Representative

Researcher

Specialist

Strategist

Technician

Volunteer

Writer

Congratulations! You are no longer unemployed or ACTIVE. You are a PASSIVE CANDIDATE and your desirability rating just went up exponentially. You are on your way.

The next order of business is to craft the perfect cover letter and update your curriculum vitae (CV) or résumé. If you already have a framework for a CV, please read through the chapter on Résumés before you send it out.

For now, work on a job description akin to what you are presently doing. Additionally, give some thought as to what you want to be doing and begin to think of ways to get involved today. The main point is to take action.

Six Review

!

ⓘ Don't get depressed. You are not a loser just because you are currently out of work.

ⓘ Create a position title based on what you are doing now while seeking your next job.

ⓘ Volunteer.

ⓘ Take a class to brush up skills or learn new ones.

ⓘ Write about what you love and get paid for it.

ⓘ Update your Linked In profile.

ⓘ Update your Résumé, but don't send it out quite yet.

ⓘ Above all – take action!

Seven - How Passive Candidates Can Create Urgency

!

The stereotypical image of a PASSIVE CANDIDATE is one who is *desirable* or *in demand*; someone that is *difficult to find*. As a result of your elevated status, your ego may tell you that you can name your own price or be more selective about opportunities that present themselves. The cliché often attached to you is that if you are gainfully employed, you must be good.

Remember what I said about being replaceable? Don't fool yourself that you are the best thing since sliced bread just because tradition says so, as your situation can change from passive to active at any time and for any number of reasons that I mentioned earlier.

Moreover, if you are a person who is actively employed yet are not yet in your dream job, then really, underneath it all, you are more akin to an active candidate. It's just that potential employers don't know it. You are the new breed of job seeker known as *actively passive*. You may not necessarily be looking, yet you surely do not want to miss out, and therefore, you want to hear what's available in the market should something better come along. We live in a loyal-less society both from the employer *and* the employee's perspective.

Let's say you are an Investment Banker and you get wind of an opening with a highly desirable Private Equity firm. You have secretly been thinking about what it would be like to work on the buy side. By the way, most calls or meetings that I have with Investment Bankers inevitably lead to the topic of moving over to the 'buy side.'

Maybe you are a nurse who quietly desires to work for a homecare health company that affords you the opportunity to travel the world. You may be a passive candidate, yet secretly you are open to making a change, which, in reality, makes you active.

Possibly you work in sales or marketing for a large technology company, yet confidentially desire to join a start-up.

How do you create urgency toward any of these opportunities without being labelled as *loyal-less*, or worse, *desperate,* like the active candidate often is perceived?

How do you let your dream employer know that, while you are happy in your current role, you would simply die to work for them?!

How do you overcome the caution that some employers maintain in thinking that you are more likely to back out of an opportunity due to your current comfortable status?

How do you overcome preconceived notions that you might be too expense, have higher demands or simply be too good to be true?

How do you overcome poaching policies that discourage top competitors from reaching out to you?

How do you find the opportunities when no one knows you are secretly interested in making a move?

While passive sounded great at the start, it can actually be a hindrance if you secretly want to move up and out of your current role.

I will let you in on a little secret. Times have changed!

The current market mind-set is that EVERYONE IS ALWAYS LOOKING! Remember the *loyal-less society*? Being passive is no longer a controlled setting.

HOW TO INCREASE YOUR OPPORTUNITY PIPELINE

There are ways to appear more urgent and to generate opportunity flow while still maintaining a sense of stability, security and control. Here's how:

-        Contact a Recruiter who specializes in the industry you wish to move into or whom works for firms at a different level than your current company. Explore their perspective on market opportunities, but do not give them authority to submit your résumé until you are serious about making a change.

- If you already know what it is that you dream of doing, give yourself a definite timeline to make the move. Based on that timeline, begin to take small steps toward it. Most people start six months in advance.

  o If you are at an industry conference, make a point of running into someone attending who works for a company in the area you are interested in. Ask them about their experience and satisfaction with their current role.

  o Contact someone at a mid level in a company you are interested in. Ask them to join you for coffee. Express your curiosity as to their market position and growth strategy. Their focus is in an area that you might want to explore in the future.

- If and when a Recruiter contacts you about an available position that interests you, respond in one of the following ways:

  o "I am not looking, but I like to know what's out there."

  o "I am happy in my current role, but am always willing to listen to what is available.

○ "While I am not planning a move, I might consider the right opportunity."

- If you are serious about being more active in your job search, implement a self-imposed deadline and make a plan. Put the plan (with milestones) in your calendar.

  ○ Expect up to six months from exploration to offer.

  ○ Identify the industry you desire to be in. If it is the same, then determine the company that you might wish to work for in that industry. For example: do you want to work for Microsoft or Google, or would you rather work for a tech start-up?

  ○ Is your goal to work in another city? Would you consider a lateral move? Larger firm? Smaller? Will your own firm move you?

  ○ Make a list of five desirable companies in the field/sector/industry you wish to be in.

  ○ Revert to early advice about contacting prospective interests.

  ○ When you meet someone who is in a job or with a competitor that interests you, ask them about *their* journey. This may lead to further contacts and introductions.

Be active in your communications and connections. Be open to opportunity. Reach out selectively toward what you truly desire. You are operating from a position of strength, yet do not be untouchable because of it.

SEVEN REVIEW

!

① PASSIVE CANDIDATES ARE DESIRABLE.

① MOST PASSIVE CANDIDATES FALL UNDER THE NEW CATEGORY: ACTIVELY PASSIVE.

① IF YOU ARE NOT ALREADY IN YOUR DREAM JOB, YOU ARE CLOSER TO AN ACTIVE CANDIDATE.

① SEEK OUT EXECUTIVES IN THE INDUSTRY OR COMPANY WHERE YOU WISH TO WORK. ASK THEM ABOUT THEIR JOURNEY.

① ANSWER RECRUITER OR COMPANY CALLS.

① KNOW WHAT TO SAY TO MAINTAIN DESIRABILITY AND OPENNESS.

① BE AVAILABLE!

EIGHT - SKELETONS IN YOUR CLOSET

!

When I meet with job seekers like you in my office or on the phone, it is not what they are telling me that I am interested in. It is what they are NOT telling me that I want to know. I want to know if you have any skeletons in your closet, and so does the Hiring Manager.

Are you 'too good to be true?' Are you just a bunch of 'hot air?' Is there a REASON you were fired from a past job? If you parted ways for internal 'political' reasons (such as there was a new head of the group that came in and he/she wanted their own people), how did that situation unfold? Why didn't they keep you if you are so good?

Hiring Managers (whether they are the Head of HR, a member of the team you will be working on or the CEO him/herself) will want to know that your record is clean. They will check, so be honest when they ask you about your current situation.

If you do not have a clean record, it is not the end of the line for you. It just means you have to be upfront and bring it up in the conversation as opposed to hoping they don't find out. You have to face the skeletons in your closet head on. By doing so you will be respected and often forgiven. If you try and hide something, it will come back to embarrass you.

Here are two skeleton stories.

I was placing a recent college grad in a junior role at a leading firm. He had completed two internships at good firms during the summers of his sophomore and junior college years and was currently employed at another quality firm. The grad wanted to upgrade his situation to work for a bigger 'platform' and I was helping him. His skeleton was bony.

During the interview process this young man met with several people at the company I sent him too. He did well and was invited to visit the big brass at company headquarters. The company flew him in and he spent a day interviewing across the organization. Everything went like clockwork (which is usually what happens when someone is fast tracked). After his successful interview rounds, the company decided to make him an offer, yet first had to do a background check (which included a formal verification of past and current employment). That's when I got the call.

"Did you know that the candidate is no longer working at his current employer?"

Really! I was angry and embarrassed. I called the candidate and asked him to level with me. He had been fired during the interviewing process (he eventually admitted that he knew it was coming) and he didn't tell me *or* the potential employer because he was embarrassed and felt uncomfortable. He also told me that the senior members of his team said not to say anything. As you can imagine, not only did he not get the job, he made me look bad and made his colleagues look bad for their unethical advice to him regarding the badly timed situation. The grad went on to get a job at another firm, but now that firm is merging and he has been laid off again. Will I be helping him? Probably not, but I can assure you he learned his lesson and will never make the mistake of not being fully upfront again.

The message to you as you seek your next job is: Do Not Lie. Do not cover up your past. Bring up any situation regardless of potential repercussions. It is the right thing to do and believe it or not, as uncomfortable as it may seem at the time, it WILL work in your favour. All the college grad had to do was a) call me and tell me and I would have told the company or b) call the Head of HR and tell them his current status. Luckily for me, I quickly found another excellent candidate that my client hired within three weeks.

I have to admit I go a little overboard with job seekers now and ask them several times throughout the interviewing process if they are still employed at their firm (for those who are passive candidates – obviously an active candidate is available immediately). This situation is more common than you think. In fact, you may have found yourself in this predicament as well. I advise you to be honest and upfront and to reveal all of your skeletons.

Be honest and be positive. Own up to any mistakes and bring them up in the first conversation. Explain what happened and do not whine, beg or cry.

I know a highly decorated finance executive who was in the wrong place at the wrong time. He should have been a whistle blower, but he didn't blow the whistle and not only got stuck holding the pink slip, he had a permanent black mark on his personal report that the governing industry organization keeps on file. This executive was a junior team member at his firm and was part of a transaction to sell one company to another. Unfortunately, it was suspected that certain team members told the company that they would do something positive for the company in exchange for getting the deal. This something was against industry rules and not allowed to be promised. Unfortunately for the finance executive, the company complained and water flows downhill. Several people on the team were fired and he has had to explain the situation in every interview since. However, this did not stop him from getting offers of employment. I advised him to bring it up right away and explain the situation. He was given the benefit of the doubt for being an upstanding finance executive and landed his next senior role in only a few months.

Remember the job seeker I told you about who did something unintentionally wrong by covering for another employee? It got him fired immediately even though his intentions were noble. I advised him to reveal this infraction during the first interview for the next position he applied for. It will likely take him longer to find the perfect position, but it would be much worse for him if the potential employer found out on its own. We spent time discussing how to present this unfortunate occurrence (ideally in person) so that he is portrayed as a team player as opposed to a breaker of rules.

My career advice to him was to alter his focus within his industry by moving over to the supplier side of the business so that he could stay in the field he loves and use his many years of experience to get considered. He followed the advice in HIRED! and I am happy to report is in the middle of interviewing for a mid level role with two supplier companies that serve organizations similar to his previous employer.

Maybe you have a vacation booked and you know that you will not want to start your new position for a month. Do not go through the entire interview process to the point of getting an offer and then spring your month long adventure on your new boss. Pick a time along the way to transparently share your plans and ask if it is OK. It is more than likely that if you are the one they want to hire, you will get the offer *and* your vacation.

If you are a woman and are thinking of having children soon, or something else unrelated to your ability to handle the job for which you are being considered, this is not considered a potential skeleton. It is the cycle of life and you have every right to have a child whenever you determine it is right for you. I personally experienced this during my career. I had my first child and within a month of returning from maternity leave, I was pregnant with my second. At the time, my previous industry consisted primarily of men in management and I have to admit I was very hesitant to tell my boss that I was pregnant again. I think I waited until I was almost 6 months along, or after bonus season, to reveal my state. Times have changed and employees are protected so much better today. I would not recommend waiting like I did. You have every right to have a family whenever you so choose.

Did you know that there are many things an employer cannot even ask you? Some of those questions include:

Age * Race * Religion * Political Affiliation * Marital Status * Sexual Orientation * Are you a U.S. Citizen * Disabilities * Do you drink, smoke or use drugs * Are you pregnant

Just do a search on Google "questions an employer cannot ask you" or consult an attorney if you have any concerns about a situation that gives you concern. It is a good idea to know what an employer cannot ask you so that you are not caught off guard.

I do not want to make you suspicious but I do want you to be prepared. Sometimes interviewers will use what I call the 'friend approach' to entice you to reveal more about yourself than you necessarily need to.

The interviewer may want you to feel comfortable, like two friends talking, so that they get you to convey more than you may have intended. Remember, their main goal is to find reasons not to hire you. It is their job on the line if they make a mistake and they want to head off a bad decision at the start. Additionally, remember that if you are the one that brings up any skeletons in your closet and if you accompany that skeleton with a solid explanation, you actually make the interviewer's job easier and they will be grateful.

So as it relates to the friend approach, be aware of questions that start with *we* or *tell me a story*. The more comfortable you feel, the more you may reveal and the more reasons you may give the interviewer to *not* recommend you. Decide in advance what you want an interviewer to know about your personal life, know what they can and can't ask you and remember to always bring up any occupational skeletons that might affect your candidacy. The company *will* conduct a background check on you.

I know the CEO of a company who was sanctioned by the SEC for a personal investment faux pas. His company was involved in a round of funding to keep the lights on and he was at a crossroads as to whether he should bring up the sanction to potential investors. Would they find out? Could he sweep it under the rug and explain it away if it did come up? Fortunately for him, he brought the sanction up early in discussions, followed by a logical explanation and guess what, the company received a very important strategic round of funding and is thriving.

I know an accomplished salesman who was a top producer at his firm. His issue was that he liked the ladies - so much so in fact that he had an affair with the daughter of his boss. His boss found out and he was fired. The salesman learned from it and vowed never to venture down that road again. However, in his next interview he had to answer as to why he had been fired. The salesman brought up the indiscretion early in the interview and explained that he and an employer's daughter began dating and, unfortunately, while they continue to care for one another, the co-worker was not in favour of the courtship and he was phased out as a result. No, he is no longer dating her and while sometimes love has a way of finding us, he is determined to stay away from love in the workplace, even if it's once removed. He was soon hired again.

I know a woman in public relations who had an affair with her boss. She said he was using his power and the promise of advancement to woo her. She saw it as a chance to climb the corporate ladder. Either way, they were both guilty and she was fired. When the question of her termination came up in her next interview, she was quite clever in her reply, which went something like this.

"I was in a high pressure position which included a great deal of travel and entertaining. I travelled often with the head of my division who volunteered that he was not happy in his marriage. There were many late night meetings that led to after hours discussions and, unfortunately, one thing led to another and we were involved. Unfortunately for me, I was let go and he is still at the company. While I did feel taken advantage of, I vowed never to let the workplace cross the line into my personal life again." The PR executive was hired at an even larger firm and she has never mixed business with pleasure again.

Only *you* know if you have skeletons in your closet. And only you know if they need to be revealed. My recommendation is to be upfront and honest before the potential employer finds out. The transgression may not be as bad as you think and if you are honest and forthright, chances are it will be overlooked, forgiven or explained away. Unless, of course, it is a felony of some sort. You should consult a lawyer if you have any questions or concerns.

Eight Review

!

- ⓘ Be honest no matter what.

- ⓘ If you have a skeleton in your closet, make sure that *you* bring it up.

- ⓘ Be positive.

- ⓘ Be familiar with questions that are taboo.

- ⓘ Do *not* be defensive.

- ⓘ It is what you are *not* saying that the interviewer wants to know.

- ⓘ The interviewer wants to cover himself by not making a bad choice.

- ⓘ A background check will be conducted. Take the initiative and reveal any skeletons beforehand.

- ⓘ Don't mix business with pleasure in the workplace.

NINE: RELATIONSHIPS AND COMMON GROUND

!

Some people are natural born communicators; they can talk to anyone about anything. Others can get up in front of a crowd and deliver a flawless speech. Certain individuals can go into a room full of strangers and never feel alone.

Most people are none of the above.

This chapter is designed to give you the strategies you need to establish common ground and build a rapport with each person you connect with along the way. The tools are built to give you confidence in your communication abilities and to increase the connection between you and the person who is interviewing you.

Whether it is an email, a voicemail, a video interview or a face-to-face meeting, you first must learn how to establish rapport with the person. How do you do this? By finding common ground.

You have found a company that you wish to be considered for based on your dream job criteria. You have further found the head of the division that you wish to work with and you have secured his/her email. Next task – research. Go to the company website and pull up the person's profile. You find that he went to college in Chicago. You are from Chicago. Common Ground #1. You read that he runs marathons. You like to run. Common Ground #2. You read that he used to work for a competitor of your last firm. Common Ground #3. Whatever tidbits of information you can find that dovetail with your background or interests, use them in your initial interaction. By mentioning commonalities, you are establishing rapport with the person reading your email or interviewing you face to face. When I speak with job seekers I always try and find common ground with where they currently live. Throughout my career I have been able to build instant rapport from this one small tidbit alone. I grew up on the East Coast, which connects me to all east coast job seekers. I worked and lived in Manhattan, which connects me even more with a certain type of east coaster. My entire family is from the Midwest and I raised my family on the West Coast. I have also travelled to many countries in the world. I think you get the gist of what I am saying. From location, I move on to educational background and personal interests. By the end of the first couple of minutes, I have found two to five common ground topics that I can expand on as needed.

Once you have established a source of common ground, the inevitable result is that the person you are dealing with will relax and like you. When someone likes you, they are more willing to open up and share information with you that can help you with your quest. The more someone likes you and opens up, the more you need to – LISTEN.

THE ART OF LISTENING

Listening is the #1 skill you can develop and that will help you as you seek your dream job. By listening, you are more likely to establish additional common ground and a meaningful relationship with the person you are in communication with. As you listen you will learn, and the conversation will more likely develop effortlessly.

Listening does not mean waiting for the other person to stop talking so that you can talk about yourself. Listening does not mean trying to impress. You must approach this very important tool with an attitude of service. Keep asking yourself how you can be of service to the other person. See the interaction from their perspective and ask yourself how you can help make the conversation more interesting and valuable for them.

At one company I worked for earlier in my career, I often travelled with the head of the firm to visit clients in other U.S. cities. It was not fun. Why? Because it was all about him. We would head into a meeting with the CEO of a prospective client company and the first thing my firm head would do was talk about who he knew. Trust me, that gets old very fast. I would do my best to interject questions that led back to our reason for being there, which was to learn about the company from the CEO's perspective. It didn't matter. Before the CEO could answer, the head of my firm would jump in again about how he did some famous financing or how his art and wine collections were bar none. We never left those meetings with a signed engagement letter.

When you listen with an attitude of service, an unspoken bond occurs. If your communication is focused on what you can do to make the other person's life easier, then chances are they will come to rely on your help, which may end up in a job offer at your dream company. How do you develop this attitude of service? You ask questions. Your questions can range from interest in the person's career path, their vision for their company, their ultimate goals or how they balance their life. What you offer in terms of skills and core competencies can be woven into that conversation without you needing to do the bulk of the talking or selling. A short answer to their needs is where your value comes in and if you are seen as providing assistance and service to the other person, you will come across as someone who adds real value as opposed to someone who is simply delivering a sales pitch.

ATTENTIVE LISTENING
When you listen, be sure that you are present. What does this mean? Direct eye contact, head nodding when you agree, slight movement of the eyebrows and corners of the mouth as appropriate to

demonstrate your understanding. Lean forward slightly as the other person is speaking and rest your hands on the table so that they are in full view. These sorts of subtle gestures will show the other person that you are not just listening, but that you are hearing them.

A tactical listening skill that you can employ is the use of the *pause*. When the other person is done speaking, count 'one one thousand' slowly in your mind before you answer. This short pause will demonstrate that you are considering what the other person has said and that you are giving thought to your response based on what they have said. This tactic will serve you well as opposed to your having already rehearsed what you want to say in your mind and not letting a split second go by before you get to the important part of the conversation – you. In using this silent gesture, you will soon see that your colleague becomes more interested in what you have to say. Caution! Once the tables turn, remember that your information should always be wrapped in the attitude of how you can be of service to the other.

As you are doing this, be sure to pay attention and be receptive to what the other person is doing as well. Are they looking at you? Are they facing you straight on or are their legs crossed and their arms crossed in front of their chest? Do they look at you when they speak or are they distracted? Look for non-verbal cues when they speak and also how they react when you speak.

EMAIL

When it comes to email communication, we do not have the advantage of seeing the other person's demeanor, delivery or reaction. We only have words on a page. So use your words wisely. How do you do this?

1. Respect the fact that the email recipient's time is valuable and therefore, make your email short.
2. If it is a new relationship, establish common ground quickly and then get to the point.
3. Be professional in your delivery, but not too formal.

EXAMPLES

1. Dear Tom, Alex Martin, a colleague of mine who knows you from business school, thought that it might make sense for us to meet. I am the highest revenue producing sales person for Company Z and I am seeking to make a change to a larger platform. I would welcome the opportunity to buy you a cup of coffee and learn how you grew your career. Should you be available, I could meet you any morning next week. Sincerely, John Smith

2. Dear Allison, I wanted to congratulate you on your new position as CFO for Company B. I am the controller for my current firm and am interested in making a shift. Should you have a few moments next week, I would enjoy the opportunity to meet with you to learn more about Company Q and your plans for growth in your department. By the way, I noticed on your company bio that you have run an ultra marathon. I have only run regular marathons but am hoping to run an ultra next year. I would be curious as to how you trained for such a challenging event. I look forward to connecting as your schedule allows. Sincerely, Janet Jones

In example one, John established a mutual colleague as the common ground. This is one of the best ways to have your email answered. As you research the person you are going to contact, see if anyone you know knows them. You can search LinkedIn for relationships as well as you may find crossover. In example number two, the common ground was finance and running. In each example the job seeker was able to promote himself or herself without being obvious. The approach was focused on interest in the other person's experience, journey or vision. The job seeker was simply offering up a skill set within their primary interest of learning more about the email recipient.

NINE REVIEW

!

- ⓘ RESEARCH AND FIND AN AREA OF COMMON GROUND

- ⓘ WHEN YOU ESTABLISH RAPPORT, YOU ARE LIKED

- ⓘ WHEN YOU ARE LIKED, YOU ARE HEARD

- ⓘ LISTEN WITH YOUR FULL ATTENTION

- ⓘ REMEMBER TO PAUSE BEFORE YOU SPEAK

- ⓘ USE EYE CONTACT AND ATTENTIVE BODY LANGUAGE

- ⓘ INITIAL EMAILS SHOULD ESTABLISH COMMON GROUND, BE POIGNANT AND INQUISITIVE

Ten - Social Media

!

Social Media has exploded in recent years and it seems that everyone is online everywhere. Whether it's Facebook, Twitter, Google Plus, LinkedIn, Pinterest, WordPress, FourSquare, Instagram, Yelp, YouTube and more; we are being bombarded with invitations to share our lives online. While this can be fun and interesting, it can also be harmful to your dream job quest if you do not handle your social media world carefully.

If you are on Facebook (aren't we all?) I recommend only using it for friends and family. I am not a proponent of 'friending' any business associates on Facebook. Why? I do not believe that they need to see pictures of my new puppy or my son's graduation. Mixing business with pleasure is not recommended. On the other hand, there are over 800,000,000 Facebook users so it wouldn't hurt to post a message that you are in the market for a position and would appreciate any referrals of openings that your Facebook friends may know at companies in your area of interest. Just don't turn your Facebook into your job search portal or personal blog about issues of controversy. Also, be sure to manage your posts and keep in mind that if your account is public, then potential employers will be looking at it. When I wrote my first novel, I posted a few messages about it on my personal Facebook page. I then created a page for my novel and told my Facebook friends that I would no longer be posting information about my novel on my personal page. I directed them to my Facebook novel page if they cared to follow me.

BTW, if you are looking for a fun chick lit read, my novel is available. It is called "No Time For Love" by J.B. Miller. I am happy to say that I have sold many copies around the world and would love to have you as a reader too! Here is the link. http://www.amazon.com/Time-For-Love-J-B-Miller/dp/0988474832/ref=sr_1_1?ie=UTF8&qid=135257376 1&sr=8-1&keywords=no+time+for+love+by+jb+miller It is also available on IBooks and Barnes & Noble.

In general, on all Social Media, your intention should always be to appear professional and to present yourself in the most favorable light. Photos or videos of you rocking out at Coachella might not be the best idea. Ranting about an old boss on Twitter may also not be the wisest use of your time. When girls go through Sorority Rush at college they are told to make their Facebook account completely private (for their eyes only) until Rush is over. Why? Because the girls already in the sororities are looking on Facebook for any odd behavior. Remember what I said about Hiring Managers trying to find a reason NOT to hire you? You can rest assured that they are looking too.

The one social media site that you absolutely must be on is LinkedIn. LinkedIn is indeed the most powerful network for finding jobs, connections and, even more importantly, for being found. Do you have any idea how many opportunities you are missing if you don't have a presence on LinkedIn? Ok, maybe you already have an account, but does it emote quality?

LINKEDIN

KEY ELEMENTS TO A SUCCESSFUL PROFILE

1. When you set up your LinkedIn account you are asked to fill in each area of your profile. Fill out a complete profile. Be clear, succinct and results focused.

2. Be Truthful.

Did you read the story about Scott Thompson, the Yahoo CEO who claimed that he had a Computer Science degree when he did not? Not good! What he could have said was "studied at" or "attended" as opposed to claiming the degree (that is of course if he took some or any classes at that particular institution).

I know an executive whose is a heavy hitter in media sales. He was recently ousted after a battle of wills with his boss. He told me that he walked out, yet I heard from someone I know inside the company that he was fired due to this conflict. He asked me to help him with find his next career move. My first line of action was to counsel him to be completely truthful. He had a parting of the ways with the head of the firm and he was let go as a result. It's that simple. Conflict happens. You have to own up to the reality of the situation and move forward from there. For this particular executive, he was still angry and didn't take a moment to reflect before approaching everyone he came across, telling him or her about how horrible his past boss was and that he needed a job. Unfortunately, he was appearing bitter and desperate and I had to stop him - fast.

"Tom, you are asking every neighbor and dad in your kids class if they can help you get a new job," I told him when we met for coffee. *"It's time to put away the chip on your shoulder and operate from a position of helpfulness and value."* I had to explain to him that his diatribes and insistent requests for job leads were not a good idea. It's crucial to network, but never ever appear desperate. If you have been fired, you first need to reflect, get a grip and proceed humbly and professionally.

The executive and I sat down and I encouraged him to focus on what he wanted to do next in life. Did he want another job in media sales management? While that is what he did for most of his career, it wasn't all that he had achieved. The more we talked, the more it became obvious that he hated media sales! So we looked at another job that he had had as part of a technology company where in he built out their social network and advertising platform.

He loved that job! Based on that experience, we crafted his résumé to reflect the skill set that he had garnered from all of his positions in such a way that they spoke to his new area of interest - technology start-ups who needed to build revenue streams. We rewrote the synopsis of each of his jobs to more accurately reflect the direction he wanted to go, rephrased his LinkedIn profile, loaded his new CV onto his LinkedIn account and strategized as to who he should invite to connect with him based on his new career goals. I suggested that he load the document onto his LinkedIn profile so that he would have a better chance of being found on the worldwide professional network. We also worked on a role that he could enter as his present position, now that he had parted ways with his recent firm. An advertising client who had heard about the break contacted him and asked for his professional advice on their media strategy. I recommended that the executive immediately list his current position as Consultant.

Remember to create a position for yourself if you are currently out of work and seeking your next opportunity. Your first listing on your LinkedIn profile should list whatever role you are in as 'present.' Never say something like "seeking the next opportunity" as your current position. If you give enough thought to what you are doing on a daily basis, you can come up with a position that you are presently undertaking.

3. Enter A Summary Of Your Abilities

This is your elevator pitch. Do not enter information about what you are looking for. Why? Because an interesting opportunity may be looking for you! If you write something like *"interested in expanding my sales experience with a leading Fortune 500 company"* and a very exciting start - up that just may go public in the next year or two is interested in you, they will likely pass you by. It is better to put a summary of your skill set and key accomplishments. Make it brief and make it action oriented.

Example: *Sales Manager and revenue generator for technology based companies pursuing increased market impact. Track record of increasing enterprise sales revenues 500% within first 12 months.*

Example: *Merchant Banker with over 15 years experience completing 30 M&A transactions and 40 financing transactions totaling $30 billion in value. Client development, origination, negotiation and execution. Focus on industrial and energy sectors primarily.*

4. List your WORK EXPERIENCE in reverse chronological order. Start with your current position and go back in time up until college or high school.

Include the company name, your title, dates of employment and a line or two about the position. If

144

there are monetary or percentage based accomplishments that you can add, please do so. Bullet points are also acceptable. In essence, you are pulling from your résumé in the work experience section.

If you have a title that can be improved upon, you might consider doing so, as long as it accurately reflects your duties in the position.

Example: If you are a waiter or waitress, you may be a *"Lead waitress and Director of Customer Satisfaction"* as opposed to *Waitress*.

Example: *Senior Book Buyer of Women's Fiction* rather than *Buyer*.

Note: If you are a Consultant, you may not want to list every consulting job you have ever had. Your job history should not be too long. Choose wisely as to how many jobs you wish to include. Choose the most notable assignments out of the many you may have had.

If you change jobs every year, I suggest not listing as far back as high school or college. Ideally you want to have 2-7 jobs, depending on how long you have been in the work force.

5. List your EDUCATIONAL EXPERIENCE. Do not forget the dates – well, in most cases.

I know an institutional finance executive who is in his 60s. He looks a lot younger than his age, but a fact is a fact. On his LinkedIn account he does not report the year that he graduated from college. Therefore, one cannot count backward and figure out his age. I personally do not have a problem with this. The world is not supposed to discriminate against age, but the reality is - it does! On the other hand, if you are seeking a Board of Director role, then age can work in your favor. It is up to you, yet from my perspective it could be more advantageous after age 60 to omit your age so that you are not passed over before even being considered. Your intention is to get the in person interview. Once you are in that seat, you will impress that employer with your many years of excellent experience and well-rounded perspective.

If you did not graduate from a college or university, yet attended classes, you should list your educational experience as *attended* or *studied at*. If you did graduate, list the degree(s) that you earned and any academic, athletic, political or volunteer involvement you were associated with. Also list all academic, athletic or arts honors you may have received. Do not go crazy with associations. Just list the most visible or recognizable.

6. Upload Your Résumé? Not Always

In general it is a good idea to upload your résumé to your LinkedIn account so that potential employers can learn more about you. However, I am not always in favor of this. If you are currently out of work and looking, then by all means upload your

CV. If you are currently employed, then it is likely not wise as your current employer can see that you have done this and may become suspicious. Rather, in the Settings section, you can check "career opportunities." This is a more subtle way of letting potential employers know that you are willing to be considered. You can also choose to allow Open Link and InMail. I have an Open Link setting, which means that anyone can email me for free. I am a Recruiter so I want to connect with many people. You should do the same. If you do not have an Open Link account, then people will have to pay a monthly fee to gain enough InMails to email you. If your LinkedIn Profile is not interesting enough with a quick 10-second glance, then they won't bother. In my LinkedIn Account, I do not choose "career opportunities" because I already have my own firm and do not wish to work for another. You should definitely check "career opportunities" whether you are an active (looking) or passive (open to opportunities but not actively looking) candidate.

7. Connect

Once your profile is complete, it is time to invite others to connect. Don't go crazy with this because if you do you will receive an email that requires you to put in a person's personal email in addition to your connection request. In other words, you will be considered spam. You want your rating to be 5-star, so don't spam. Also, do not invite your best friend and high school sweetheart to connect with you on LinkedIn. You can do that on Facebook. LinkedIn is for your professional life, so keep it that way.

I recommend reaching out to 10-15 people in your industry who you know or have a tangential association with (you worked at the same company, they work for a competitor, etc.). Ask them to be added to your network. In your settings, allow them to see all of your connections as well because they may find that you have people in common which can only help your networking efforts. If you can't remember who you know (even tangentially), then go to the People Advanced Search and enter in a company you know and it will list the employees at that company.

8. Test the Waters

Once you have built up some connections in your industry, use the same advanced people search to find 5 informational interview contacts. You can enter company type by keyword, or exact company name, title of person (recommend junior or mid level (Associate/VP, etc.). Invite them to connect with a brief note.

"Hi Tom, I am a junior account executive for P&G. Would love to get your perspective on the market landscape if you have a few minutes to connect. Thanks, John." Keep doing this until you connect with 5 potential allies. Keep the request short and to the point. Be pleasant and accommodating.

Types of messages you're willing to receive

MESSAGES
- (•) Introductions, InMail and OpenLink messages (Recommended)
- ( ) Introductions and InMail only
- ( ) Introductions only

OPPORTUNITIES
- ☑ Career opportunities
- ☑ Expertise requests
- ☑ Consulting offers
- ☑ Business deals
- ☑ New ventures
- ☑ Personal reference requests
- ☑ Job inquiries
- ☑ Requests to reconnect

ADVICE TO PEOPLE WHO ARE CONTACTING YOU
I look forward to learning more about your role at your company.

Include advice on your availability, types of projects or opportunities that interest you, and what information you'd like to see included in a request. See examples.

Save changes or Cancel

9. Mentor Mining

Once you have gained a few relationships and maybe even had a call with one or more of them, it is time to reach out to potential mentors with the same message.

For the mentor relationships, search for someone high up in an organization in the industry where you want to work.

"Mr. Jones, I am a senior programmer, most recently with Google. I was hoping I could buy you a cup of coffee and gain your perspective on wise career choices in the programming sector. If you are inclined, possibly we could have a short visit one morning next week. I look forward to connecting with you."

Sincerely, Sarah Miles

Repeat Steps 2-4 until you have gained a small handful of contacts that you can speak or meet with.

Follow up each day. Don't be pushy, always defer to the other person's schedule.

Always say thank you. Don't talk too much.

Listen, listen and listen.

If you are a big user of Social Media, you might consider signing up for www.hootsuite.com, which allows you to manage all of your social platforms, including posting messages to all of them from one location.

10. Upload a Professional Photograph

Recruiters and Employers will want to see what you look like. Make sure you look professional. A job seeker I was helping in the wholesale retail space had a picture of himself partying on a boat. Not a good idea. While he doesn't need to post himself in a suite and tie, a nice button down shirt and combed hair was the better choice.

I also do not recommend a photo of you with your family. Your LinkedIn profile is about you – keep it that way.

11. Industry

When listing your industry, make sure it accurately reflects your background or the tangential industry you are seeking to join.

12. Keywords

Use keywords throughout your profile that will increase your ranking when you show up in an industry or skill based search. For example, if you are in sales, enter words such as 'sales leader,' 'global sales,' 'revenue,' and other words that show that you are at the top of your game.

13. Open Mail

It is worth reminding. Check the box for Open Mail so that anyone can email you through LinkedIn. Many Recruiters pay large monthly subscription fees to be able to email candidates directly; they always appreciate it when they can email someone for free!

Remember that Employers and Recruiters use Social Media to find candidates that match their requirements. They especially like to find diamonds in the rough or passive candidates that are not officially looking. This is why it is so important that, if you are an Active Candidate, you have figured out a current position and listed it as 'present.'

OTHER SOCIAL MEDIA SITES

Google+
Ning
Meet Up

Facebook
Twitter
Tweetmyjobs
Pinterest for Job Seekers
Gadball
Jibe
BeKnown
Ziggs
Jackalope Jobs
Klout

By the time of this publication, there will likely be many more! Explore them, consider them, but take caution that you are selective and targeted in getting your name and intention into the social fabric of the Internet. As long as you have LinkedIn, you are golden. Anything after that is either gravy or burnt toast.

A final reminder: Employers and Recruiters will be scouring the Internet's social media sites for your profile. Stay focused and consistent. Everything you post or upload is a reflection of your professional self. Keep your personal dalliances to a bare minimum (unless on Facebook, which I recommend that you primarily use for your personal life). Take care that you are putting forth your best impression, as Hiring Managers will be watching. Use the privacy settings on most of the social media networks that you use, other than LinkedIn, which should be public.

Ten Review

!

ⓘ Keep all of your social media profiles professional or use privacy settings

ⓘ The number one social media site to be on is LinkedIn

ⓘ Explore the plethora of job seeker social media sites, but be selective

ⓘ Employers and Recruiters will be watching

- When you fill out your LinkedIn profile, enable the display in settings that says 'career opportunities.' This is a way to let potential Employers and Recruiters know that you are interested in hearing about opportunities.

- On your LinkedIn profile, allow receipt of InMail. This way Recruiters and Employers can contact you directly without bothering you at work.

- Do not post more than one job referral request on Facebook or other personal social media. Focus your professional job search on LinkedIn, as this social media destination site is focused 100% on business networking.

Eleven – Getting Found

!

We've discussed posting your résumé on targeted job boards, utilizing certain aspects of Social Media (primarily LinkedIn), working with Recruiters and targeting certain executives within companies that you might want to work for or learn more about.

We've discussed the value of networking with others, but not to the point of stalking, and you have been encouraged to get out into the community where potential contacts might gather.

All of these methods will help you get found.

Additional ways to get found include attending 'meet ups,' which are a new form of networking event that take place across the country according to interest.

Let's say you want to be an entrepreneur. In the San Francisco Bay Area there are entrepreneur 'meet up' group events every week. Some are free and others require a small donation at the door. They are held in restaurants, company lobbies and meeting halls. You can simply search them, see who is going and decide if it is for you. You can also start one yourself.

http://www.meetup.com

I know an Insurance salesperson who was in charge of customer experience. He was recently downsized out of the firm where he had worked for many years. After going through the self-discovery process, he realized that his true passion was being a motivational life coach. He was used to improving the customer's experience, which translated well into improving the life discovery experience. One of his key sources of new clients, speaking engagements and referrals has come out of his attendance at 'meet ups.' He is now a key organizer of 'meet up' events and had developed a client list longer than he can handle.

BE AVAILABLE

As an Executive Recruiter, too often I have to chase down candidates. It makes me crazy when a job seeker tells me he is going to send me his credentials and then I have to keep asking. What does that make me think? They are shopping around or they aren't really interested. On the other side of the scale, when a job seeker hounds me daily, I begin to lose interest and consider them potentially desperate and slightly unprofessional. If I am thinking these things, and I am on your side, imagine what a Hiring Manager is thinking should your approach be akin to one of the above.

Be prompt in your communication. Do what you say you are going to do. Do not act self important, even if you are a CEO. Be available within a normal workday. Be pleasant, thankful and professional. It sounds simple, yet you would be surprised at how many people lack these basic skills.

Check your LinkedIn account on a regular basis. Most Recruiters and many Employers use LinkedIn to contact potential hires. Do not leave them waiting. If you are not interested that is one thing. Yet, if there is a possibility that you might be interested down the road, at least respond.

Keep in contact with colleagues, but again, do not stalk them. Do not appear desperate. An email now and then letting an associate or past client know what you are up to is welcome. A request to be hired is not. Be exciting in your updates and thank them for letting you know if any roles come up that they believe you may be suited for.

Do not blindly apply to job postings. Find the company contact and email them directly, referencing the position.

Do not load your résumé onto every job board. Choose the industry job boards that relate to your dream job only. Be selective. Additionally, if you load your résumé onto many of the subscription job source services, you are now in their system. While companies can search your skill set and you may be 'matched' for a particular opening, it is quite likely that they may have already passed over you and you will have no idea of knowing. It may be better to search the posted jobs on those sites, find the executive who runs the division and contact her directly. At least this way you are in control of the relationship and are aware if you are to be considered or not.

Attend community network events such as Rotary, Toastmasters or Meet Ups.

Go to conferences in your industry. Many of these charge nominal amounts to attend. Visit the booths of companies that interest you. Make direct contact and follow up with a thank you and ask for their referral within the company.

NEVER send your résumé unless it is requested.

Make your LinkedIn profile professional and enticing.

Finally, conduct a search of yourself on the Internet. Make sure that your online presence is consistent throughout.

Eleven Review

!

ⓘ Be available

ⓘ Check your LinkedIn email

ⓘ Respond promptly to inquiries

ⓘ Attend community gatherings

ⓘ Go to industry conferences

ⓘ Be selective in uploading your résumé to job boards or résumé services

ⓘ Search yourself online and make sure that all references are professional

TWELVE - THE COVER LETTER

!

A cover letter is much more than an introduction that accompanies your résumé; it is your voice in the ear of a potential hiring manager.

Maybe you are a job seeker who is simply networking. Or possibly you are inquiring 'cold' as to whether a particular company has an opening. You may be applying to a posted position on an industry job board or corporate web site. You may be responding to a Recruiter's inquiry. While we will cover a variety of wording styles to address your particular situation, you need to know that it really doesn't matter the circumstance. What *does* matter is that your unique voice comes across.

I have seen thousands of cover letters and have edited more than I can count. The bottom line is that you need one that reflects your interest or inquiry in a concise and cordial manner, with you coming through.

A cover letter is almost like a handshake and a pleasantry before the meeting starts. It's an invitation for the hiring executive (whether that be a person in Human Resources or the CEO of the firm) to review your credentials.

Sometimes a cover letter is all you need. Again, it depends on the situation. We will cover that too.

If you are contacting someone for an *informational interview* would you send your résumé? No. You send a cover letter. If you were responding to a job posting, would you send a cover letter? Yes, and your résumé.

If a company or a Recruiter contacts you, do you send your résumé? It depends.

As you can see, every situation is unique, yet in any and all situations, you still need a cover letter, which is an introduction or an invitation to get acquainted.

What format should you use? What works best in today's fast paced, have no time world?

"If I get a résumé in the mail, I think the candidate must be from another generation"

— Head of Human Resources, leading financial company

If you read the quote, you already know that *snail mail* is something of the past. Hiring Managers of today are much more technologically savvy than those of yesteryear. As a job seeker, I recommend you get with the program.

As an Executive Recruiter serving one of the highest paid industries in the world, I can tell you with certainty that I have never received a 'hard copy' of a cover letter or résumé in the mail. Not once. Why?

I tell every job seeker to email me.

Not only is email more efficient in a world where turn around time has been reduced to hours or minutes; it shows that you are current and sensitive to someone's time.

My number one recommendation on format or sending method: EMAIL!

The challenge you will have is finding the email of the person you need to send your introduction to. There are many tools to help you do this. Here are a few:

1. Look on the company website for the name of the person you are seeking. If you do not know their name, search titles, divisions or executive management to find it. If you can't find it or don't now, then Google the name of the head of the department you are interested in. Example: *Head of Sales, Name of Company, contact.*

2. Look on the website (or as a result of your search) for the email string. Usually it is first letter of first name followed by full last name @ company name.com. Or, it's first name.last name @ company name.com.

3. If you are still out of luck, go to Zoom Info or Spoke and type in the name of the company. You will get a list of names and emails and you will find the email format.

4. Once you obtain the person's name and title that you are looking for, you can begin to craft your cover letter!

Remember, a cover letter is your personal invitation for the Hiring Manager to learn more about you and to review your credentials.

Recall that we discussed how little time Hiring Managers have in the world of *I need it now*, so it is your job to make *their* job easier by crafting a very concise and cordial cover letter that will get you noticed and that will make you stand out from the crowd.

How do you do that?

GET TO THE POINT

By now you have figured out that you should not waste the recipient's time. You may be the most amazing candidate in your industry, but I promise you that if you send a lengthy cover letter filled with how great you are and how you are the perfect person for the job, you will fall from grace quickly.

In fact, it is my opinion that you shouldn't attach a cover letter to your email at all. Your email *is* your cover letter! Let me say it a different way. Your cover letter is your email!

When I get an attached cover letter nowadays, I immediately think 'amateur.' I do not want you to be that! I want you to put your best professional foot forward and here is how you do it.

SUBJECT LINE:

The subject line can make the difference between ending up in the Inbox or the Delete Folder. Make it relevant.

If you are seeking to network, you can put any of the following:

- Inquiry
- Connecting
- Request for meeting

Any of these subject lines should elicit a response and lead the recipient to open your email or read the first few lines if they have the preview pain enabled in their email configuration.

If you are replying to a job posting, you can always reply to the website or job board directly, or, as I recommend, find the hiring manager and email them directly instead. This way you stand out from the crowd. In this particular situation, the subject line can say:

- Responding to position of Programmer (include reference number) or whatever the role is
- Interest in programming role (include reference).

Please note that if the job posting says no emails or calls, then you must respect this - initially. You can always follow up directly later on should you not receive a response from your application. Do not assume that a 'no reply' means a rejection. It might be as simple as landing in the spam folder. You have another reason to follow up and you will learn how in HIRED!

MAKE A CONNECTION

Before you contact the human resources executive, head of the department you wish to work for or person who leads the division who is posting the position of interest to you, you must do some research so that you can make a connection.

You need to look for something in common with this person.

One way to find a camaraderie is to search LinkedIn and view their profile (another good way to find the person you are seeking by title), and look at where they have worked, what college and/or grad school they attended, where they went to high school, where they live, etc. Find a commonality and mention it in your email cover letter. Here is an example of common ground:

I graduated from Boston College in 2010 and see that you also attended BC. I too was a member of the entrepreneur club and heard that you were very influential in its growth.

THE HEART OF THE LETTER – SUMMING YOU UP

You need to sum yourself up in as few words as possible. I repeat, as few words as possible. If you don't waste the Hiring Manager's time, they will look upon you more favourably and will at least review your credentials. Moreover, if you apply for that which you are qualified (not over, not under) then they will appreciate your understanding of the role.

BUZZWORDS

In your cover letter email, it is OK to use buzzwords. If you do use them, do so sparingly. Plain, concise language is always best. Let's start by looking at a sample of buzzwords that you shouldn't use, and ones that are OK to use. This is only a very small sample, but you will get the idea. The message you should take away from this is to be authentic, real and plain in your communication. Go ahead and use a buzzword or two, but please try to avoid too many and make sure you don't use words that your intended audience may not understand.

BAD BUZZ WORDS

- "That being said"
- "Best of breed"
- "At the end of the day"
- "Proactive"
- "Thinking outside the box"
- "Synergy"
- "Paradigm"
- "Metrics"

- "Solution"
- "Ramp Up"
- "Win-win"
- "Value-add"
- "On the same page"
- "Customer centric"
- "Best practice"
- "Big picture"
- "Buy-In"
- "Cross platform"
- "Supersede expectations"
- "Going forward"
- "Enterprise"
- "Silo"

GOOD BUZZ WORDS

- "Bandwidth"
- "Sticky" or "Stickiness"
- "Coverage universe"
- "Collegial"
- "Collaborative"
- "Ranked"
- "Maintained"
- "Built"
- "Established"
- "Led"
- "Developed"
- "Negotiated"
- "Structured"
- "Diligence" "Due Diligence"

- "Identified"
- "Analyzed"
- "Transparent" (starting to be a bit overused)
- "Core competency"
- "Inquire"
- "Incremental"
- "Reach Out"
- "Reach back"
- "Ping"
- "Vertical" "Sub vertical"
- "Crowd Source"
- "Cloud Approach"
- "Emotional Capital"
- "Intellectual Capital"
- "Streamline"
- "Incentivize"
- "Skills transfer"

SAMPLE COVER LETTERS

EXAMPLE:

Dear Mr. Johnson,

I am a senior programmer responsible for creating the code for my company's global sales database. My firm focuses on crowd sourcing and I am grateful to be part of this growing industry trend. My latest review focused on how my programming has saved the company several hundred thousand dollars in outsourced fees.
I would be very interested in meeting with you to learn more about your plans for your programming

division at (NAME OF COMPANY) as we move into the New Year. I am confidentially considering a change to a more sales focused firm. I also noticed on your corporate bio that you are a mountain climber. Have you climbed McKinley yet? I too love the sport and am training to climb Everest.

Thanks very much for your time and I look forward to connecting with you as your near term schedule allows.

Best,

You
xxx-xxx-xxxx
you@email.com

EXAMPLE:

Dear Tom,

I wanted to reach out to you to see if you had a short window to meet in the coming weeks. I am a Strategic Consultant in the energy industry, currently assisting Company Z with their roll-up strategy. I noticed that you are looking for a Business Development Executive and I believe that my 10 years in mergers and the intellectual capital this role requires, may be suited for such a position. I would be happy to forward my credentials in advance of our discussion and look forward to connecting with you. BTW, I noticed that you are from Madison, New Jersey. I grew up going to the Nautilus Diner. Have you tried their double chocolate cheesecake?

Sincerely,

You
xxx-xxx-xxxx
you@email.com

In each of the above examples, the candidate is describing what he or she does, mentions something in common and submits a call to action. The inquiries are concise, personal and professional. As you craft your cover letter email, be sure to include these elements:

1. Who you are and what you do
2. An accomplishment of note
3. A common ground data point
4. An interest in them and their firm
5. A call to action: response, meeting, telephone call

Twelve Review

!

ⓘ Research an actual *PERSON* to send your Cover Letter or Inquiry to.

ⓘ Do **not** send a formal snail mail Cover Letter. Send a concise Email instead.

ⓘ Make a personal connection.

ⓘ Use buzz words sparingly.

ⓘ Get to the point.

ⓘ Include your contact information after your name.

ⓘ Always send a thank you!

Thirteen - Your Résumé

!

Your résumé is you on paper; in reverse chronological order with your most recent (or current) position listed first. In as little as a page, this document should do its job and represent you so well that you get the meeting. Securing an in person interview should be the goal of your résumé.

When crafting your résumé, you must be sure to represent the best summary of you, as you will not necessarily be sitting in front of the reader of this document.

How long do you think a Hiring Manager, Recruiter or Human Resources person spends looking at your résumé? Do you think they read it word for word, reveling in your use of adjectives and action verbs?

In all reality, you have about 10-15 seconds to grab the attention of the reader. Your résumé is less than an elevator pitch, so it had better be good.

NOTE: Another name for résumé is Curriculum Vitae, or C.V. for short. I recommend calling your résumé a C.V. in your communications. It is the highest form of professional label given to this document and immediately portrays you as someone 'in the know' and operating at an elevated, qualified level.

As an Executive Recruiter, I receive hundreds of résumés every week. I accept résumés that are unsolicited, referred, résumés from candidates that I have sought out and résumés I search from targeted service providers. My daily 'to do' pile becomes quite large, quite quickly.

When I receive résumés via Email, I am grateful because then I can 'control find' them for certain keywords of value. The paper résumés usually get put into a pile that I rarely go through once I have placed them there.

HINT: Email your résumé, but not until it is requested.

WHO ARE YOU?

Your résumé should start with your contact information at the top. Further in this chapter you will see different formats, yet regardless as to whether you align your document left or justified, you should place your contact information at the top.

Your contact information should include Name, Address, Telephone (ideally mobile number) and Email.

WHAT DO YOU WANT?

The next element of your résumé is the OBJECTIVE or SUMMARY or OVERVIEW. This initial segment is a short synopsis of who you are or what you want. Regardless of the way you put forth your objective, you should be promoting what you can deliver.

EXAMPLES:

WHO YOU ARE/SUMMARY or OVERVIEW: Seasoned sales executive with track record of increasing consumer sales beyond firm expectations.

WHAT YOU WANT/OBJECTIVE: A senior sales management role that promotes global growth and revenue milestones.

If you know the position for which you are applying, by all means craft your objective or summary to answer the call.

EXAMPLE:

SUMMARY: Institutional Salesperson with track record of increasing tier one accounts by 400%.

SUMMARY: Top ranked Research Analyst with ability to predict top stock performers within the energy and cleantech sectors.

OBJECTIVE: A position in retail management that allows me to apply my 15 years in apparel expansion and revenue growth.

NOTE: I have reviewed résumés with both approaches. I personally tend to favor the summary or overview as it states and subtly promotes your strengths rather than asking to be considered. I do not think that you need to include both an objective and a summary or overview. However, I do not think you can go wrong with either one or both. It is a matter of personnel preference.

Following the objective is the EXPERIENCE section. This is the meat of your résumé and in it you tell the prospective employer,

WHAT YOU HAVE DONE

If you haven't already figured it out, your résumé is your sales pitch and you need to make sure that your pitch is catchy, concise and encourages a 'call to action' on the part of the reviewer. This needs to come through in the experience section as you are not only telling the prospective employer what you have done, but what you can do for them.

I am not saying that you need to write your résumé as though you were pitching a box of cereal or a new house cleaner, yet you do need to make it enticing, aesthetically pleasing and easy to follow.

In terms of aesthetically pleasing, I do not mean the use of fancy fonts, swirly headings or elaborate borders. You do not want to detract from the content of your document. Rather, you want to draw attention to its substance. The way to do this is to produce a clean and confident looking document that allows the reader to quickly scan the format and subconsciously conclude that you are an organized professional.

NOTE: If you are a graphic designer, interactive game creator/programmer or if you are in a very creative industry, then all bets are off. You would be best served creating a résumé that highlights your particular skills within the genre of your profession. However, I still recommend a copy of a clean résumé to accompany your creative presentation.

- I like the use of bullet points in the experience section of the résumé. Ideally, the simple dots or black boxes.

  - Each bullet point should contain a line of action verbs that focus on what you have accomplished as opposed to flowery descriptives about your personality or 'people skills.' Employers want to know what you have done and what they can rely on you to do if they hire you.

Each bullet point should start with a word that describes what you have achieved or are in the midst of achieving. This is the time for you to unabashedly tout your achievements in a very factual, professional manner.

SAMPLE ACHIEVEMENT WORDS

- Led
- Compiled
- Monitored
- Performed
- Achieved
- Supported
- Participated
- Launched
- Developed
- Designed
- Executed
- Originated
- Worked with
- Cultivated
- Responsible for
- Managed
- Oversaw
- Built
- Established
- Collaborated
- Sourced
- Directed
- Completed

- Increased

You should describe what you have achieved (or are currently achieving) in no more than one or two lines.

HINT: Do your best to put all of your information on one page. I know this can be challenging, but remember, you only have about 15 seconds and you will want to make sure that the reader scans as much of your document as possible. They rarely go to page two.

I have had job seekers send me 5 page résumés. My first reply is to ask them to pair it down to no more than one page before we can begin. My initial recommendation is to do this by removing all flowery adjectives.

HINT: If you have a particular company in mind where you would like to interview, read the job descriptions for open positions that they have posted on their website and in your achievement descriptions, craft some of your accomplishments to address certain aspects of the position that you are interested in.

HOW MUCH ($$$$) DID YOU ACHIEVE?

Another component of an excellent résumé is the use of numbers and percentages. As you describe the vital achievements that you have accomplished, your résumé will jump off of the page when you assign numbers and/or percentages to those achievements. Hiring Managers, Recruiters and Your Future Boss will want to know what quantitative goals you have triumphed. Here are some examples:

- Executed over $1Billion of sell-side transactions within the Healthcare Services sector
- Increased network advertising revenues by 200% within first 18 months
- Recruited new business accounts resulting in 100% firm growth in first 12 months
- Reduced division redundancies by 300%, resulting in a 200% firm wide savings for fiscal year

NOTE TO INVESTMENT BANKERS:

If you have had a few very tough years (as many have) with few closed deals, yet several that have almost made it to the finish line, you can consider including them to more fully round out your résumé. There are many reasons why deals do not close; terms, control, terms. I often receive investment banking résumés with 'abandoned deals' or deals that did not close or did not go public. Sometimes the situation is simply beyond your control, yet you may have worked on a particular transaction for many months or for as long as a year. Include them.

Be sure to include dates and location of each position you list. Go back as far as college, unless the list is more than seven positions. If that is the case, then simply list the roles under OTHER as a company heading.

After the EXPERIENCE section comes EDUCATION. In the education section, list the degrees that you have earned. Name of college, graduating year, degree(s) bestowed, GPA if you are a more recent graduate. If you have earned an MBA, list your GMAT scores if they are favorable. See sample formats. If you are in the midst of obtaining a degree, put 'expected' and the date. If you do not have a college degree, list your high school graduation and any trade schools or educational training you have completed or are in the midst of completing.

Following education is SKILLS or SKILLS AND ACCOMPLISHMENTS OR SKILLS AND INTERESTS or simply OTHER. In this final section you can list your licenses, technical skills and personal interests as you wish them to be known. I always recommend putting in one unique accomplishment. For example: Black Belt in Tae Kwon Do, Climbed Mt. McKinley, Avid Stamp Collector, Member of Kappa Sigma Fraternity. You would be amazed how many times an interesting hobby or talent catches the eye of the reader. This section is another way to potentially create common ground without having to do any research.

Other ancillary sections that can be included if they are extremely relevant to the role you are applying for are as follows:

BOARD OF DIRECTORS (on which you serve)
AFFILIATIONS (organizations that you are involved with)
PUBLICATIONS (books or articles)

Finally, include a final section entitled REFERENCES. Under references, write 'furnished upon request.'

Congratulations! You have written your first Curriculum Vitae. Now go back over it slowly and correct any typos or grammatical errors. Also be ruthless in your assessment of flowery language. Keep it factual, active and accomplishment oriented.

If you feel that you need additional help with your résumé, you can order my critique services by following this link: http://sellfy.com/p/q3hd

SAMPLE FORMATS

Reminder: Do not get fancy with fonts. Simple and clean is best. Make sure you are consistent with any use of bold or italic throughout. See samples.

Be sure to include answers to the following:

- What did you do that is notable
- How did you create efficiencies
- How did you drive revenues
- How did you provide analytical value
- Types of transactions completed, accounts serviced, etc. should be included as a separate attachment

BOOK ANTIQUE

Your Name

Full Address (no P.O. Box please)
Telephone Number and Email

Objective

Simple sentence or two about what you are seeking and what you have to offer. I also like to call this OVERVIEW.

Experience

Job Title and Company   **Location, Date - Present**

- Achievements and responsibilities

- Use Action words

- Site revenues or efficiencies

Job Title and Company   **Location, Dates**

- Achievement and responsibilities

- How did you drive revenues, increase accounts or provide efficiencies

- Did you complete transactions? Describe them

Education

Educational Institution   **Location, Dates**
What you studied and what degrees you have earned.

Skills and Interests

List all relevant skills you may have that associate with the position you are applying for. I also like to call this section OTHER. You can also include your personal interests.

References

Furnished upon request.

TIMES NEW ROMAN

JOHN SMITH
1230 Seventh Avenue, #19E
New York, NY 10001
xxx-xxx-xxxx
jsmith@email.com

EXPERIENCE

COMPANY   NEW YORK, NY
Vice President – Division   2009 – Present
- Achieved....
- Produced....
- Compiled and disseminated

COMPANY   NEW YORK, NY
Associate – Division   2006 – 2009
- Led...
- Created....
- Sample projects include...

COMPANY   DALLAS, TX
Associate Director – Division   2005 – 2009
- Managed...
- Designed...

COMPANY   NEW YORK, NY
Title– Division   2003 – 2005
- Led...
- Created....
- Sample projects include...

COMPANY   NEW YORK, NY
Title – Division   2001 – 2003
- Led...
- Created....
- Sample projects include...

EDUCATION

COLLEGE
NAME OF SCHOOL WITHIN COLLEGE   Date of Graduation
Degree
Scholarship

SKILLS & PROFESSIONAL LICENSES

List technical skills and licenses

186

ARIEL

John D. Smith

10 Jones Lane • San Francisco. CA 94111• xxx-xxx-xxxx• johnsmith@gmail.com

Objective

    To apply my 10+ years in ...

Work Experience

01/2011   Company X, San Francisco, CA United States
Director, Head of XXX

- Advise companies.....
- Consult with...
- Secured revenues of X
- Promoted company brand...

06/2009 -   Company B, New York, NY United States
09/2011   *Vice President, XXX*

- Developed .....
- Programmed....
- Expanded firm footprint....
- Marketed....
- Achieved 100% increase in company revenue

04/2006 -   Company Q, New York, NY United States
05/2009   *Vice President, XXX*

- Grew company salesforce....
- Increased firm revenues 40% in first year
- Recruited as member of quality assurance committee....

02/2005 -   Company Z, San Francisco, CA United States
04/2006   *Associate, XXX*

- Supported management....
- Responsible for completion of....
- Served as....

Education

    College. Graduation Date
Degree

    New York University
MBA

Skills

    List technical and personal

References

    Furnished upon request.

There are many different ways to format your résumé. Style is a matter of preference. Scan the code below to see many sample styles. Choose the one you like best. The key is to have all of the pertinent information you need in order to grab the attention of the reader.

ADDITIONAL
RÉSUMÉ FORMATTING SAMPLES

Thirteen Review

!

- Always put your contact information at the top of your document

- Choose between objective or summary/overview. You don't need both

- Use action verbs to promote your achievements

- Use numbers and percentages to emphasize accomplishments

- Use ancillary sections sparingly and only if relevant to the position you are applying for

- Choose a style and stay consistent throughout; no fancy fonts or swirly borders

- You have created your first Curriculum Vitae: C.V. Congratulations!

FOURTEEN: TYPES OF INTERVIEWS

There are several different types of interviews that you may encounter in your quest for your dream job. While the face-to-face interview is the ultimate deciding meeting(s), you will encounter alternative methods as well.

THE COVER LETTER

I mention your cover letter as the starting point of your interviewing process because it holds a great deal of importance. This communication opens the door to an interview and should be crafted such that it elicits a positive response.

THE RÉSUMÉ INTERVIEW

Believe it or not, your résumé (Curriculum Vitae) is your first actual interview. It is you without your voice, yet still a representation of you. Your résumé should be crafted to put your best foot forward on paper and make the best impression possible. The chapter on résumés will give you a detailed overview of what you should have in the document. There are also QR codes that will take you to additional résumé samples that you are free to use as a template for your own résumé.

THE TELEPHONE INTERVIEW

I have many client companies that make it a practice to interview over the telephone first. This is akin to a screening.

There are many reasons for a telephone interview initially, including simply not having enough time to meet every first round interview face to face. Companies also need to narrow the pool of candidates to a manageable number. It's not unlike applying to college. Your grades and scores are your first interview. If you do not meet the minimum requirements, it doesn't matter how good your essay is or how many hours of community service you have performed. The same is said for your résumé.

As an Executive Recruiter, I often initially rely on the telephone interview due to logistics such as considering someone who is in New York when I am in San Francisco. For junior roles, I tend to want to speak with someone on the telephone first as well because I get so many interested candidates that I couldn't possibly meet them all initially.

Personally, I like the telephone interview as I can have my spread sheet open on my desktop for immediate reference, I can sit comfortably and I don't have to worry about my appearance.

In the telephone interview you want to come across at personable, comfortable and humble, yet you want to highlight your achievements. As the interviewer goes through your background, make sure to weave in a specific accomplishment in your answer as often as you can. Do not drone on, make it concise, yet conversational. Answer the exact question and end with a question about them if appropriate. Use pauses before answering and don't ever cut off the interviewer. Hear what they are asking as opposed to being anxious to say what you have to say. Repeat back what they say every so often so that they know that you hear them correctly.

EXAMPLE:

Interviewer: *How much time do you spend on each transaction?*

Pause.

You: *I can imagine you would want to know if I spend my time wisely. In my practice, I usually have three to four transactions going on at the same time. While I give them all equal attention, due to the nature of the structures, some take a few weeks and others can take as long as six months. I had one joint venture that took four rounds of negotiations up to the Board level. We completed it successfully and collected a six-figure fee, yet the many iterations took many late nights and weekends. I was glad it all worked out. Sometimes we have to stay the course to see something through even when it may look dismal at any point along the way.*

In this example, you let the interviewer know that you heard her question, you gave a deeper understanding and insight into what she might be getting at, you gave concrete examples coupled with a success and you demonstrated your work ethic. All of this in the answer to one question!

VIDEO INTERVIEW

My recommendation is to avoid this type of interview at all costs. No one looks good on Skype or via Video Interview Systems. At the very least, I believe it is hard to establish a feeling of connection with the interviewer. I also think that mannerisms can be misconstrued. If you look down or away on a video chat, it might be interpreted as avoidance rather than pondering your answer. If you maintain eye contact 100% of the time, it might make the interviewer uncomfortable. The interviewer will undoubtedly be examining your background surroundings as well to see what your work environment is like. What if you get interrupted or a large noise occurs in the background? The whole idea of video interviewing is distracting and distorting.

My son had to undergo a video interview via Skype to be considered for a special camp on the other coast. I had to keep telling him to look into the camera and position the computer so that he was in the center of the screen. I have a very nice desktop with a high-resolution camera yet the connection was not high definition so neither party looked ideal. The audio lag time was annoying as well.

I simply do not like video interviews and recommend against them unless that is your only option. If you must be interviewed via video, make sure to smile, relax and dress in a professional manner. Avoid stripes or loud colors, as these may be distracting as well. The one good thing about a video interview is that you can wear shorts or jeans because the interviewer won't see your entire outfit when you are sitting down!

IN PERSON INTERVIEW

Ideally, this is what you are pining for. I have devoted an entire chapter to the in person interview.

FOURTEEN REVIEW

!

ⓘ YOUR COVER LETTER IS YOUR INITIAL
INTERVIEW

ⓘ YOUR RÉSUMÉ IS YOUR FIRST FORMAL
INTERVIEW

ⓘ THE TELEPHONE INTERVIEW OFFERS
FLEXIBILITY

ⓘ AVOID THE VIDEO INTERVIEW IF YOU
CAN

ⓘ YOUR GOAL IS TO SECURE THE FACE
TO FACE INTERVIEW

ⓘ BE RELAXED, CONVERSATIONAL AND
FOCUSED

ⓘ LISTEN ACTIVELY AND INSERT AN
ACCOMPLISHMENT INTO YOUR ANSWERS

ⓘ DO NOT RAMBLE

Fifteen: The Main Event: The Interview

My job as a Recruiter is so much more than reviewing résumés and submitting credentialed paperwork for consideration. Like many experienced Recruiters, I can sum up a candidate on paper in about 30 seconds. But a good résumé alone does not get someone hired.

My next step is to meet with the person (if logistically possible) or have a lengthy and deep telephone conversation, after which I decide if I will recommend them.

If I do recommend them, I am committed to securing the interview for the job seeker. Once I get them the meeting, the biggest challenge of my role as Recruiter and Coach becomes helping the candidate put their best foot forward so that they nail the interview!

How do you interview? Do you have any idea of your style, your approach and your plan? Trust me - you need to prepare.

You need to know yourself so well that you can field any question that is thrown at you.

I know a college student who was recently interviewing for a paid summer internship at one of the biggest companies in the world. She has good grades and a major that fits with the position she was applying for, which got her to the first round. But once she was in the round, it had nothing to do with her grades and scores. It had *all* to do with her emotional intelligence.

What do I mean by

EMOTIONAL INTELLIGENCE

The ability to gauge the interviewer's style and personality, adapt to the audience and deliver your answers in an informed, confident and comfortable manner - all characteristics that make up emotional intelligence.

Assessing emotional output or 'reading the signals' is a key factor in being successful in an interview.

It is great if you have good grades and you went (or are going) to a top college. That's a *door opener* starting point. But if you start the interview with a limp handshake, I don't care how good your grades are - you will be judged poorly.

You may feel that you are starting from behind because you didn't go to a top college or you had poor grades or maybe you didn't even finish. Yet through your ability to present a background that solves a problem for the hiring company, or your developed skills and experience that fit the position you are persuing, you landed the interview. Add in a firm handshake and excellent eye contact and you just jumped a rung on the hiring ladder.

ⓘ Tip: Emotional intelligence is extremely important in your interview.

This particular college student had five back-to-back interviews and a lunch. Based on her performance during these meetings she would get scored by the company and then compared to the other 10 potential Interns interviewing for that particular day.

INTERVIEW PREP

She prepared in advance by reading up on the company and their marketing strategy, including both failures and successes based on the companies market share. She came up with two ideas for improving previous failed marketing attempts and two ideas for expanding successful plans. She memorized key players in the company and reviewed their top competitors. She searched for recent news about the company so that she had something current to refer to if needed. Basically, she did her homework.

You must do your homework before your interview ever starts.

Here are some online tools that will help you look up companies and learn more about them.

www.wikipedia.com

- General company information that is added to and updated/authenticated by the public

www.hoovers.com

- Detailed company information plus financials, filings, board members, competitors

www.google.com

- Search any way you want to about the company (use " " for exact phrases or words, use AND, OR, NOT, etc.)

- Lesson on performing a Boolean Search:

  o http://websearch.about.com/od/intern etresearch/a/boolean.htm

www.zoominfo.com

- Detailed information about companies, plus current news, current and past employees, competitors

www.linkedin.com

- Overview of companies plus links to employees who work there and their backgrounds

www.glassdoor.com

- Information posted by employees about companies they work for (or have worked for) (anonymously)

WHAT TO WEAR

The company was known for dressing casually and emitted a laid back feel in work environment. Jeans or black slacks would be acceptable. In fact, the company told her this. However, having superb emotional intelligence, the college candidate knew how important first impressions were. She opted for a knee length skirt and flats, a light colored blouse and button down sweater to appear slightly more professional, yet comfortable. Add in nice smelling shampoo, light make-up and subtle jewelry, a conservative purse, a breath mint while waiting, and bingo! She was ready.

I tend to advise people to over dress as opposed to under dress no matter what. Men should wear suits. If the company always dresses in jeans, then wear kakis or black slacks and a dark blazer with a crisp button down shirt underneath. You can always take off the blazer and drape it over your arm. Otherwise, always wear a suit.

MEN'S INTERVIEWING OUTFIT IDEAS

Women should always wear a knee length (or below the knee) skirt, low heels and a blazer with a crisp blouse underneath. If the company tells you 'business casual,' still opt for upscale. If the company dresses in jeans, wear a button down sweater instead of a blazer. Small earrings and a light necklace (I usually do not wear a necklace as I want people to look at my face) and maybe a subtle bracelet if you like them. I tend to wrap a long strand of pearls around my wrist to act as a bracelet.

I do not recommend a watch. Why? You don't want to absently look at it during your interview. Trust me, almost every person I interview who wears a watch subconsciously looks at their watch. And I don't think it is because I'm boring or they want to leave. They want the jobs I fill and are otherwise very attentive. Looking at your watch is a habit and I don't recommend it during your interview. It sends the wrong message. Your smartphone has a clock on it. So does your car, most lobbies and anyone on a street corner.

I am not a big proponent of the boxy look. I believe that women who think they need to dress like men because they want to be taken seriously are not being true to themselves. If you are a woman, it is OK to be a woman. In fact, you should be proud of your womanhood and dress as a woman.

I often tell female candidates to dress conservatively which I describe as black slacks or dark skirt, a crisp blouse that is conservative but has a little of their personality thrown in, and a tailored dark blazer (minus the big shoulder pads). Heels of low height, light on the make-up and jewellery, clear nail polish (or French manicure) and hair tailored. Think crisp and professional.

WOMEN'S INTERVIEWING OUTFIT IDEAS

THE INTERVIEW BEGINS
While waiting in the lobby for her interview to begin, the Paid Intern Candidate sat tall with legs uncrossed, knees together and ankles crossed to the side. She did her best to appear relaxed (even though her stomach was doing summersaults!).

When I am being interviewed for a potential new client account, I never sit while waiting in the lobby. I prefer to meet my potential new account eye to eye from the start. However, you may be very nervous, so sitting and taking a few deep breaths can actually help prepare you by relaxing you and eliminating shaking. Either way is fine.

As soon as the first interviewer appeared, the college student smiled and stood up. A firm handshake and direct eye contact, followed by, "Hi, I'm Jennifer," completed the introduction.

That was it.

The interviewer took over from there and brought her to a room where she would meet with five company employees, followed by a lunch with a sixth.

Make sure you look the interviewer in the eye and do not be the first one to avert your eyes. Extend your hand and offer a firm handshake (not crushing, not limp, not fingers only, not two handed). Hold your portfolio/folder/résumé/purse/smartphone or whatever you have with you in the other hand. One shake is fine, not multiple.

The interviewer led the interviewee down a hall filled with other workers in cubicles. The interviewee smiled at those who caught her eye and made a comment to the company representative.

"People really look engaged."

"Yes, we like to think they enjoy their work."

And on they walked.

BODY LANGUAGE DO'S AND DO NOT(S)

Your body language should relay confidence, energy and attentiveness. When you walk, stand tall and have a briskness to your step. When you sit, face the interviewer straight on. As you answer their questions, lean forward and rest your hands on the table. Do not hide your hands, it gives an impression of covering up.

If your phone rings or vibrates, ignore it!

Do not wear a watch.

Pause before you speak.

Smile often.

Nod in agreement.

Do not touch your nose during the interview. Do not rub your eyes or your neck. Do not spit when you speak.

Do not cross your arms in front of your chest, this demonstrates that you are closed off to the conversation.

Don't interrupt.

Don't slouch.

Stand up, shake their hand and thank them before you leave.

The unspoken question that an employer really wants to know the answer to is – will I enjoy working with you?

You may think you are the most likeable person on the face of this earth. Maybe you were on the football team in high school and rushed the most yards in the history of the sport. It's just that when were in the locker room, you regularly forgot to put on deodorant and, well, to put it bluntly, you may be lacking in personal hygiene.

Your personal habits are a big part of your interview, whether you want to believe it or not.

I interviewed a candidate who wiped his nose with his hand at least thirty times during our visit. I wanted to offer him a tissue or a napkin, but I didn't have one handy and he must not have either - or else he didn't believe in them. At the end of the meeting, I did shake his hand, but I can tell you for certain that I headed right to the bathroom where I practically emptied the soap foam container into my hands in order to eliminate the germs.

When you are in an interview, please do your best to keep your personal habits in check. Don't wipe your nose with your hand. Use a tissue or a handkerchief and be delicate about it.

I once interviewed a very senior level executive who had a résumé that seemed perfect. Good thing I agreed to meet with him in person to assess his credentials, because as soon as he sat down, I knew something wasn't right. We met at a local coffee shop seated at a small round table. The first awkward thing he did was pull up a chair next to me instead of across from me. Invasion of personal space is not good. Keep a table of some sort between you if it is your first meeting. You want the interviewer to feel comfortable too. If they invite you to sit in two arm chairs nearby that create a more comfortable living room style, that's fine, but don't be the one to introduce too close of a proximity before you even begin.

Pay attention to your body language. You do not want it to knock you out of the running!

BE A PROBLEM SOLVER

Research the company. Find challenges they may have on their plate that your skills can help to provide a solution for. The challenge does not have to be grand; it just needs to relate to what you offer.

When I was an Investment Banker, I spent many hours researching the amount of cash that public companies had on their balance sheet. I knew that if they had less than three quarters worth of operating cash, then they risked their stock price dropping because investors would not believe that they had staying power. Once I found these companies, I contacted the CEO to schedule a meeting to learn more. Many times I was referred over to the CFO, but I never started there. I always started at the top.

 TIP:

When you contact a prospective company, start at the top. Now the top might not be the CEO necessarily. It depends what you are aspiring to do within the organization and how much experience you have amassed in your career thus far. However, the top might be the head of a department or team or division. Decide where you want to be and contact the head of that particular area.

Once I sat down with the CEO or CFO (many times both) I asked many questions about the business, their personal outlook for the business and their opinion as to how they were planning to fund on going operations. I remember one biotechnology company that was in the research and development phase of a cure for cancer. They had many phases to finance before they even got to the point that they could develop a drug, test a drug and ultimately patent it. They needed LOTS of cash.

What did I bring to the table? I was the problem solver!

After listening attentively and learning more about the business, I offered several financial structuring solutions, combined with sources of capital with certain levels of risk/reward. Each type of capital infusion had advantages and disadvantages and I explained them all in detail.

After much discussion we agreed that I would bring a handful of investors to meet with them, each of who represented a different type of capital infusion. We eventually settled on the most risk adverse model and I helped to negotiate the fine points of the transaction on behalf of the company.

My point in telling you this story is not that I think your personal solution will be to offer large amounts of cash to the company you want to work at, but rather, that you will come to the table with a solution to a problem that you might have found during your research - a problem that you help provide a solution for.

I know a very smart college student who wanted to go into finance. He was majoring in Economics, with only a minor in Business. Initially he was being passed over for the on campus interview pre selection process due to the fact that he was not a Business major. He knew, however, that one particular company he wanted to work for had a blossoming global expansion underway, and for that application for consideration, he phrased his interest a little differently. It went something like this.

"I look forward to meeting with you when you visit campus the week of October 5th. While it is my understanding that leading companies such as yours primarily focus on Business Major undergraduates for internship consideration, I believe that my experience brings a unique perspective to the role. I made a calculated decision to major in Economics and minor in Business. Why? I believe that we live in a global economy. It used to be that what we do in the U.S. had an effect on the rest of the world, basically ending there.

However, with the Euro, global wars and the advance of technology, we have become, in essence, a smaller financial community, sharing and reacting to financial dynamics throughout the world. We no longer are the only center of commerce. In my Economic studies, I have developed a global perspective as it relates to finance and the economy. I believe that companies need to look beyond the spread sheet to understand the worldwide potential of their business. While my minor in Business has given me the foundation for financial modelling, I believe that my global Economics perspective will add a more unique perspective and can add balance to the accounting functions that make up the bulk of the finance interns that you hire. I welcome the opportunity to meet with you to discuss my qualifications."...

He ended up with offers from three global Investment Banks, two of the largest technology companies in the world and three of the largest global entertainment firms. He took the technology company internship during his Spring Semester and one of the Investment Banks during the summer. When he and I last spoke, he had full-time offers from both following graduation.

This college student found a problem and became the problem solver. How? He found companies in the three business segments he was interested in; Investment Banking, Technology Services and Entertainment, and offered a global perspective to dovetail with each firm's ultimate goal of global expansion. He targeted companies that were focused on the big picture, but still stuck in the small picture by only hiring accounting type interns. He helped them see that by hiring an intern with a different focus, they could move toward the big picture in a non-threatening way.

As for the college student who did her homework on the technology company and made sure that her interview was professional, personal and solution focused? She secured the paid summer internship! Halfway through the summer internship she was offered a full-time position that was set to begin after she graduated from college the following year!

No matter what stage you are at with your career, whether you are a student or C-level executive, how you are in the interview can make or break your chances.

Do your homework, listen, be attentive, dress sharply, pay attention to body language and come prepared with solutions and examples that support your strengths. Relax and be confident – you are ready!

FIFTEEN REVIEW

!

① DEMONSTRATE EMOTIONAL INTELLIGENCE

① DELIVER A FIRM HANDSHAKE

① DRESS LIKE A PROFESSIONAL

① PAY ATTENTION TO BODY LANGUAGE

① RESEARCH THE COMPANY PRIOR

① INCORPORATE ACCOMPLISHMENTS AND SOLUTIONS INTO YOUR ANSWERS

① RELAX AND BE CONFIDENT – YOU ARE READY

① ALWAYS SAY THANK YOU!

SIXTEEN – THE HOW, WHEN, WHERE TO FOLLOW UP

!

Following up can be very tricky. Every one of my clients has a different style when it comes to following up. Some like me to follow up the very day they get back to me regarding a candidate.

"Did you tell them we are interested? What was their feedback?" This type of follow up is what I call the *'gotta have 'em'* follow up. It's when the person following up wants the person so badly that they lay their cards on the table immediately.

I had a VP interview at one of my client firms and within an hour of him leaving, the head of the office called me to say that he had probably pushed too hard. He had been looking for a while to fill the role and he finally had the person he wanted to hire right in front of him. He had interviewed so many candidates that he simply knew it right away. Unfortunately, this approach scared the candidate away and he decided to stay at his firm for the time being.

On another occasion, I was doing my best to convince a Managing Director to consider a senior position with the firm I was representing. He was so concerned about his interest getting out that he would only allow communication via texting. I would text him and he would not text back for over a week sometimes. Did I text him every day, every hour, every minute? No. I waited. It was tough to wait and to convince my client that he was still on the burner, yet I knew the sensitivity of the situation and I was determined to respect it. It took almost a year to get him on board (the longest out of anyone I have ever placed!), but he is happy and it all worked out, as it should.

How do you know when to follow up with a prospective employer? The short answer is, it depends.

Now let's look at the longer answer.

Let's say you emailed an introduction, an inquiry or an offer to meet for coffee and you did not hear back for a week. Give the recipient at least a week to respond. I recommend 10 days, yet a week is not unreasonable. There is a chance that your email landed in the spam file or was deleted unintentionally. While I recommend waiting just under two weeks to follow up, I absolutely am in favor of following up.

I often tell job seekers that just because I do not have a role that fits them today, I likely will soon, so please check back with me. I do my best to give them a realistic follow back timeframe based on their timing and mine. The ones that follow back to me always get my attention. So yes, do follow up, but just don't pester and never appear desperate. It's a fine line to walk, especially if you have been out of work for sometime and you, quite frankly, may be desperate. Still, control your emotions and invoke the balance of patience and persistence.

Hiring Managers want you to follow up. Why? This way they know you are interested and motivated to pursue the opportunity. So how do you follow up if you send your cover letter email and hear nothing for more than 10 days? You send another email. It can go something like this:

Dear Mr. Jones,

I wanted to check in with you to see if you had interest in meeting for coffee next week. It is possible that my initial email did not reach you.
By way of background, I mentioned that I was interested in learning more about your role at Company X. I work in a similar department at my firm and am seeking to make a change. I look forward to hearing back from you and can make myself available any morning next week.

I also would be happy to forward my C.V. if you think it might be helpful.

Sincerely,
You

I know a job seeker who follows up with me every one to three days. Even though I give him an update (which often has not changed), tell him that I will get back to him as soon as I have next steps and thank him for his patience, I invariably receive a voice message and/or email the following day. If you are working with a Recruiter, you must be patient. Recruiters are very busy, but they want you to get the interview and ultimately, the job, as much as you do. The Recruiter knows their client and they know how much to bug them or leave them alone. If you are working with a Recruiter, contact them every two weeks. In your communication, you do not have to ask them if they have an update as they most likely will have already told you that they will let you know when they do. What you can do is provide additional substantive information that might be helpful to the process or let them know of your upcoming availability to meet with the hiring company. I suggest an email over a call as you will be more likely to receive a faster answer.

If your follow up is with the company that you just met with or interviewed with, send an immediate thank you. If you hear nothing back, again, wait seven to ten days and make the follow up brief. I suggest an email first and then seven days later if you have not heard back, you can leave a voicemail.

1. FOLLOW UP VOICEMAIL:

"Hi John, I just wanted to check in to see if there was anything else that you needed from me or if you would like me to meet with other members of your team. I just closed a $10,000,000 deal with our largest customer so all is well, yet I am still very interested in continuing our conversation. I look forward to hearing back from you and will make myself available according to your schedule. Feel free to give me a call back at xxx-xxx-xxxx or via email at tsmith@mail.com. Thanks and take care.

Pertinent information in the follow up:

- Additional information of interest
- Do not ask if they got your last email or voicemail
- Looking forward to continuing our conversation
- Leave name, telephone number and email

Sixteen Review

!

① If you have an in person meeting, send thank you right away

① If you hear nothing, wait 7-10 days to follow up

① Follow up should provide additional relevant information of an accomplishment and continued interest

① Do not stalk company or recruiter

① Leave your name, telephone number and email. Repeat telephone number if you desire.

Seventeen: The Perfect Voicemail For All Job Seeking Occasions

!

A voicemail is akin to art. It should be creative yet clear. The message should appeal to the listener's emotions and drive them to take action in your favour. When you look at a painting, listen to a musical score or read an intriguing book, you love to be moved, flattered or give rise to some emotional state. A voicemail is no different.

I tend to like my art like I like my voicemails – simple. I don't want too much information being thrown at me at once. I want a clear message with a little emotional element mixed in. I like an upbeat tone, yet professional. I am picky, like I am with my art.

There are three things to remember when leaving a voicemail. These vital elements should be appropriated regardless of the situation surrounding your message. The guidelines should be followed whether you are leaving a 'cold call' voicemail or following up to an in person meeting (refer to suggested follow up to in person meeting in previous chapter).

1. GET TO THE POINT

I receive many voicemail messages from job seekers every day. They vary from 'cold call' introductions, to referrals, to follow ups regarding a previous discussion or meeting. I have to admit that after hearing thousands over the past 10 years, I press delete a little too easily. Why do I do this? I press delete for two reasons.

First, my time is very valuable. When the person drones on and on and does not get to the point, I conclude that if they cannot get to the point, then they likely will not be a great candidate for the roles I am filling.

Second, I press delete if they get to the point right away. I know why they are calling and once they tell me the substance of their call, I press delete. I have heard what I need to know and I am grateful for their directness. That is, of course, unless I need their telephone number. I have to confess that I love it most when the person leaving the message gives me their telephone number almost immediately. I respect that they value my time and I almost always call them back. If I need to speak with someone who drones on and on, as soon as I get the telephone number I press delete and then I text or email him.

I have two candidates right now who call me or email me everyday. Even though I have spoken to them many times, have listened to them ramble on about how much they want the job and have told them that I will get back to them as soon as I have next steps, they continue to call. It is very annoying. I then turn to emailing my replies. I will also text, yet I do all in my power to *not* get on the telephone with them. It is not that I do not care for these people; they are smart and talented. It is simply that I have nothing more to report at their self-scheduled juncture.

If and when it gets to the point that they continue to call just so that they can download their deepest, darkest opinions and desires, I will repeat that I will get back to them when I have relevant information. If it still continues, I let more and more time elapse between returning their communication, to the point that I will not even respond until I have relevant information to share.

I tell you this so that you don't do it. Don't pester, no matter how anxious you may be for additional information. I want you to be positioned as favourably as possible with Employers and Recruiters. I want you to learn from me and from the many job seekers that I have placed in very rewarding positions.

When you do leave voicemails, remember to get to the point! Do not leave long, rambling voicemails that are pitches or diatribes or résumés. Do relay specifics such as parameters of your next communication or request for reply, your intention or interest and maybe one small piece of information that appeals to the recipient personally. This piece of information could be a referral, an element of common ground or a similar experience or location of residence.

Let me give you an example: When I contact a job seeker cold, I like to find one thing that I may have in common with them. Here are three examples of voicemails that I have left and that have all resulted in immediate callbacks.

REFERRAL VOICEMAIL:

"Hi Tom, This is JB Miller from C2C in San Francisco. Sam Johnson from XYZ thought that you and I might enjoy connecting regarding a senior role we are filling with a high profile technology company. If you would care to discuss this position, please feel free to give me a call back at your convenience. I can be reached at xxx-xxx-xxxx and get into the office most mornings at seven west coast time. I look forward to catching up. Take care."

LOCATION/EXPERIENCE VOICEMAIL:

"Hi Sandra, This is JB Miller from C2C Executive Search in San Francisco. I was hoping to connect with you regarding a mid level position we are filling with a leading consumer company based in New York. If you have a moment to reach back to me this week that would be great. I can be reached

at xxx-xxx-xxxx. By the way, I also went to NYU. It's nice to connect with others who have a similar college experience. I look forward to catching up. Talk to you soon."

COMMON GROUND VOICEMAIL:

"Hi Bill, This is JB Miller from C2C in San Francisco. I wanted to connect with you regarding a Chicago based Head of Division role that we are filling for a mid market firm. I am in Chicago pretty often on business and also have a lot of family in the city, so if it works out, maybe we could also grab a cup of coffee when I am next in town. I am in the office for the rest of the day if you have a moment to ping me back at xxx-xxx-xxxx or via email at jbmiller@mail.com. I look forward to catching up. Take care.

2. LEAVE YOUR COMPLETE INFORMATION

As demonstrated in the preceding examples, not only do I get to the point and add an element of commonality in an attempt to connect with the listener, I always leave my name, company and telephone number. I often provide my email as well in case they prefer to reply in this regard. I suggest you do the same, as often you will receive your reply via email. When you do leave a voicemail, it is wise to repeat your telephone number, including area code. If I do not mention my telephone number twice, I do put it at the end of my message and I always say it slowly. Make sure you pace yourself and speak clearly as well.

3. BE PLEASANT

I find it amazing how often I hear voicemails that sound dour, dull and downright depressing. While I am not advocating being hyper on the telephone or filling your message with cliché phrases or jokes, I do recommend that you are succinct and professional, yet also somewhat uplifting in your delivery. A tactic that I often use is to smile when I leave a message. My voice always sounds more pleasant when I am smiling. I suggest you try it too.

Have a positive, 'can do' tone to your voice, and while you do need to self promote, it should be with an air of humbleness, gratefulness and a sense of service.

Finally, remember the word 'thank you,' and use it often. *Thank you for your time* can be a bit overused. Try a variation.

I really appreciate you taking a few moments to speak with me.

Thanks for agreeing to see me.

Thanks - I know you are swamped so I will make this brief.

YOUR DEMEANOUR

I know a job seeker who calls me to complain about everyone and everything. Nothing is ever done right, nothing is ever his fault, everyone else is stupid and he is, of course, the only one who understands what is really going on or what needs to be done. If he is that way with me, the Recruiter who is trying to help him, imagine how he is on the job! I have done my best to council him to have a more positive, pleasant demeanour, yet in the end, his fall back is a negative perspective. This job seeker is always seeking; he has not lasted longer than one year in the last four jobs he has held. If he continues to refuse to self reflect, I am honestly not sure how much longer I can help him.

Be honest with yourself. How approachable are you? Are you a *know it all*? Do you seriously believe that nothing is ever your fault? Are you constantly feeling undervalued? If so, I suggest you make an attitude shift immediately. Channel the words *humble, helpful, supportive, team player* and *giving* and see if you can shift your mental state to that of a more collaborative and cohesive future employee. You will get many more interviews with honey than vinegar.

As you reflect on the three elements for a successful voicemail: Get To The Point – Leave Complete Contact Information – Be Pleasant, the following are example voicemails that you can craft according to your particular stage in the job seeking process.

SAMPLE VOICEMAILS

1. COLD CALL VOICEMAIL:

"Hi Mr. Johnson, This is Peter Daly from Company Z. I was hoping to connect with you regarding the possibility of getting together to discuss the Marketing Manager role you are filling at (name of company). I have been in marketing leadership at my firm for six years now and think that I could be of value to what you are building. If you have a moment to get back to me this week, it would be great to learn more about your plans and to share more of my background with you. I am available to meet most afternoons next week if that works for you and can be reached at xxx-xxx-xxxx or via email at pdaly@ mail.com. Thanks very much and I look forward to getting together. Take care.

2. REFERRAL VOICEMAIL:

"Hi Sid, This is Julie Tims from Company X. Brian Thompson from Company Q suggested I reach out to you regarding my interest in learning more about how you are growing your sales force at (name of firm).

He tells me that you have built an amazing enterprise. I have been the top revenue producer at my company for the past five years and am confidentially seeking to make a shift to a global platform. If you have a moment to reach back to me, I will be sure to make myself available. Feel free to give me a call any weekday after five at xxx-xxx-xxxx or via email at jtims@mail.com. Thanks and I look forward to connecting with you. Take care."

Seventeen Review

!

- ① Get to the point!
- ① Use an uplifting tone
- ① Introduce a common ground or referral data point
- ① Leave your telephone number and email
- ① Speak slowly
- ① Suggest an action item
- ① Say thank you!

EIGHTEEN – HIRING MANAGERS/EMPLOYERS

!

How do you attract top quality candidates? Is it who you know or by referral? Are the referrals incentivized? Are they via industry connections or a buddy wanting to help out a friend? Do you post your available positions on your website? Do you post your positions on industry job boards? If so, how many? How do you decide which one(s)? Do you use résumé databases to source candidates? Do you utilize an ATS (Applicant Tracking System) to keep yourself organized? Do you use Social Media? For Employers, do you utilize the service of Recruiters? Are they retained or contingent? Do you use more than one firm at a time? Do you attend job fairs? Do you reach out to targeted candidates one by one?

I don't know about you, but I am already exhausted from all of the options available for sourcing candidates. As a Hiring Manager, it is your job to find the best candidate for the job or jobs that you need to fill. You want to find the best and find them fast. Unfortunately, there is not a magic pill that will simplify all of the issues you face surrounding your recruiting needs.

The new trend in assisting employers with their recruiting needs are matching services that tout their technical matching and sourcing algorithms as a method to find you the exact skill match for the role you are trying to fill. Some of these services are good, yet have drawbacks in that they

1.   Charge the applicant
2.   Do not go beyond paper
3.   Do not advise the applicant when they have matched or have been passed over
4.   Are crowded with similar advertised positions from competing firms which means your posting may not be as effective

I placed a mid level investment banker recently who had subscribed to one of these priority services. My firm was also working with the global firm that had subscribed to the service. My firm reached out to targeted candidates who we believe fit the position criteria. We also were able to dig deep and find out what each individual truly wanted to achieve in their professional life, where they ideally wanted to reside and what their short and long term personal and professional plans were. We created a complete picture of each candidate, which took the process 'beyond the résumé.' After we gathered our short list, I submitted the candidates to our client firm. Soon after that the Hiring Manager at our client informed me that they had already passed on one of our candidates. She explained to me that he had been 'matched' through a certain job portal provider. I asked her if the candidate knew of this and she said no, it was not necessary to inform him. Poor candidate. He had no idea that he was even being considered. Imagine how much more he could have done had he known that he was 'matched' initially. I asked the candidate if he had joined the matching service and he confirmed it, although he said that he had received no interviews. Unfortunately for my firm, that particular candidate became a carve-out and we were not credited with his application. However, the Hiring Manager was grateful for our full picture of the candidate, which caused our client to reconsider him for the role.

While such services can initially appear valuable, it is my opinion that computations alone do not a person make.

I run a very successful recruiting firm. We have a targeted approach in that we reach out to candidates one by one based on who we know, who are industry contacts recommend and via specific criteria that we believe matches not only credentials, but personality and cultural fit. It takes us much longer than an algorithm, but we really know each candidate and our people get interviewed.

The reality is, many companies do not have the time to so narrowly target each and every position they are filling, so they look at the mass approach in order to garner as many qualified candidates as they can and from there, narrow down the field. They are covered in that they can report to their boss that they have narrowed down 200 applicants to 10. They must have some really good talent in that pool if it is that big. Well, not always.

I have interviewed many a candidate who looks good on paper, yet is absolutely the wrong fit for a client.

So what is an Employer to do?

Of course it all depends on how many roles you are filling, the level of the roles and how fast you need to fill them.

Without knowing your particular company or type of positions you fill, I will give you a general guideline that I believe will increase your quality sourcing 100 fold. This combination can be utilized in part by Employers and Recruiters depending on the element that fits your particular role in the process.

ENTRY LEVEL ROLES

For entry level roles, I would recommend posting on your website with descriptions that sound campus like and are not too lengthy or technical. You are competing with other top quality companies for the cream of the crop graduates. A combination of the following could help to streamline your process.

1. On Campus Interviews: Interview at the top National Universities, but do not neglect the top 10-20 Liberal Arts Colleges. These students are very well rounded, are taught how to think analytically and are empowered to pursue ideas. They also tend to be very comfortable dealing with upper management as they have strong relationships with their professors who are often leaders in industry.

2. Targeted Job Boards: There are certain job boards that are targeted toward top-level graduates. You can, of course, post on individual college job boards for free (recommended), yet job boards such as www.ivyexec.com, which attract Ivy League graduates are also a good source for high achieving graduates. Moreover, if your company or client focus is very specific, you may want to enlist a posting on one more industry targeted job board. If you do not know which one to use, you can browse the chapter on Job Boards to see if any of the industry portals look appealing to you. I recommend staying away from the

conglomerate job boards unless the position is extremely general.

3. Your Website: When you list open positions on your website, aggregator sites will pick up your postings, which will likely appear in the results of a candidates job search. Sites such as www.Indeed.com, www.careerjet.com and www.SimplyHired.com collect postings from throughout the web. Graduate focused portals such as www.Collegegrad.com, www.aftercollege.com, www.CollegeRecruiter.com troll websites for positions, and are more targeted toward candidates seeking entry level positions. In theory you are covered by simply posting on your own company website, yet perusing the targeted job boards depending on the roles you are filling can also be a solid strategy.

4. Matching Services: There are several sourcing services available that use technology tools to match candidate's skills with your job descriptions. These services are subscriber based wherein the candidate must pay to join, after which they can upload their résumé and apply to open positions. Several of these

sources are focused on particular industries. In general, I think these services can be effective for lower level roles. When it comes to filling mid level and above positions, I am a firm believer that companies are better served seeking out passive candidates with the help of a Recruiter that specializes in their industry. The Recruiter should be able to source candidates who have recently become active and those that may have been active for a longer period of time yet for which the Recruiter can find you talent from this group as well. I also believe that these services do not capture all of the top talent available. Many candidates do not want to pay for such a service and do not believe that the service is worth the cost. These candidates usually have strong industry relationships already and you will want to find them outside of such services. However, for access to more active candidates and junior level roles, I do think that such services can save you time in sourcing an initial group of potential candidates.

5.   Hiring a Recruiter: I do not think you necessarily need a Recruiting Firm to assist you with entry-level roles, unless, of course, you have many to fill or the

other methods are not producing results for you. On the other hand, a Recruiter will bring you the whole picture about a candidate, which can be very valuable. When hiring a Recruiter or Recruiting Firm, you must decide if you are willing to engage on a retained or contingency basis. You also must consider how many Recruiters you may want working for you at a time. If you open the door to too many contingency Recruiters, then you will likely not only have a hard time keeping track of who submitted what, but your efforts may get diluted in the marketplace if too many people are calling the same top level candidates. If you hire a Retained Recruiter, you will play regardless if you fill the role or they do. On the other hand, you have their undivided attention.

NOTE: If you are a global organization filling many senior level roles, you might consider the services of a global Retained Search Firm. If you are a U.S. based firm that is seeking to fill a select number of roles at any point in time, you might research Specialist Recruiters in your industry and engage their services.

MID-LEVEL CANDIDATES

For mid-level positions, I am a firm believer in utilizing the services of a Recruiter. This, in combination with posting on your website should be enough to find the talent you need. Recruiters do not like it when you also enlist the services of sourcing portals and then claim that a particular candidate has already been 'matched.' What will end up happening is that your Recruiter will make sure that submitted candidates do not use the matching service before submitting them to you. Even when you pass over someone with this matching methodology, you may be missing out on very good talent.

SENIOR ROLES

For senior roles, I am not a big believer in posting the position. These roles should be filled with a very targeted approach. Hire a Specialist Recruiter, even give them names that you would like to attract, and methodically recruit the best of the best.

When you source candidates, what tools do you use? As an Executive Search Firm President and high-level position RECRUITER, my practice is active and demanding. I cannot waste time. I am sure you have experienced the same. So how do we source candidates? I will tell you.

REFERRALS: I am constantly talking to people in the industries where we focus. I am always asking them who is considering a change and to have their colleagues call me. I always say thank you and often give small tokens of my appreciation when someone is hired. I receive no less than 5-10 direct referrals a week. These are all candidates who are confidentially seeking a change.

LINKED IN: We regularly reach out to candidates whom we do not yet know or for whom colleagues have suggested we contact. We contact them through LINKED IN because we do not wish to contact them at their place of employment. We spend a lot of time on LINKED IN and are very targeted in our approach. We know our client's requirements, cultures and personalities and are focused on finding the perfect match.

DATABASES: We use databases one to two times a year. Primarily we search them for junior roles so that we are sure that we are considering the pool of active candidates thoroughly. In the industries where my firm focuses, getting RIF'd is pretty commonplace so being an active candidate does not mean that you are unemployable. We have placed some amazingly talented people from databases.

FIRM WEBSITES: Because our approach is so targeted, we spend a lot of time on competitor's websites, determining whom the stars are, asking our network that knows them and then contacting them directly. If they are not on LINKED IN (most professionals are), then we will send an email or call them at their place of work. Our communication is more open ended to see if they have any colleagues who might have interest in a new role. If they are interested, they always tell us. We don't have to ask.

DATA AGGREGATION SITES:

We spend money each year to subscribe to a data aggregation site. We have used different sites over the years. What I like about these sites is the thorough company information they provide, including current employees, firm revenues and contact information. I have spent many a quiet evening in front of a warm fire searching industries and perusing companies on these sites for candidate ideas. This is my 'think outside the box time' and it has served me well over the years. Some of these data sites include:

www.zoominfo.com
www.hoovers.com
www.thelistinc.com
www.insideview.com
www.boardex.com
www.spoke.com

Eighteen Review

!

ⓘ Be selective with matching services

ⓘ Limit your résumé sourcing to targeted portals

ⓘ Enlist a specialized recruiter or firm

ⓘ Reach out via LinkedIn

ⓘ Ask for referrals

ⓘ Encourage current employees to refer qualified candidates – not just their buddies

ⓘ Target your competitors

NINETEEN – RECRUITERS

!

A service called NotchUp (where you can actually get paid to interview) has been bought by JobFlo.
JobFlo is a system that Recruiters use to more efficiently manage the recruiting process, including résumés, job posting, emails and follow up. JobFlo helps you get organized, format your job description, post and advertise your jobs and manage your process. If you are a Recruiter working with hundreds of applicants for any one position, a service like JobFlo might be of interest to you.

As a Recruiter, if you are not using LinkedIn, I suggest you start right away. This is the world's largest professional database and is an excellent sourcing tool for active and passive job seekers. I subscribe to LinkedIn Pro, which gives me organizational options as well as 50 new emails a month to send directly to candidates. I have placed so many people from LinkedIn I have lost count!

Know that you are competing with sites like OneWire. OneWire is for Employers only and is not open to Recruiters. The site uses proprietary parsing technology to match and suggest subscription-paying candidates for open positions. This site is focused on the financial services sectors primarily, yet I imagine will expand beyond quickly. The one good part of the site for Recruiters in this sector is that you can at least see the names of the companies hiring and then you can pursue them accordingly. If you have candidates that match particular job postings, then you can simply find the hiring manager within the company for that role and see if they might have interest in your candidate.

Airs is another company that employers use to source candidates. This particular service appears to search all of the résumé databases that the Employer subscribes to, as well as sites such where résumés have been uploaded such as LinkedIn, Ziggs and Jobster.

Other areas of sourcing candidates include Social Networking sites such as:

BeKnown
Jibe
Tweetmyjobs
Facebook
Google+ (although this has not caught on as much as expected)

Pinterest is a fairly new site and now has a segment for job seekers.

Meet ups are a great source for finding candidates. Choose one that fits the criteria of candidate you are looking for and search the members. If you find someone of interest, look for their LinkedIn or company profile and contact them. Better yet, go to the next MeetUp and meet them!

Gadball is another site where Job Seekers can create their own online profile and network with other professionals via groups and discussions. LinkedIn also has this group feature, which is a good way to see how potential candidates express their opinion or knowledge regarding industry issues. In order to sign up for Gadball, users must upload their résumés. While I do not recommend that Job Seekers upload their résumés everywhere, this can be an interesting source for industry connections. On the other hand, Gadball's appeal is general, so it does not dovetail with my recommendation to job seekers of uploading to targeted job sites only.

In terms of you being found, Manta is a good site to post information about your firm. You must be authorized and approved to list your company on Manta, which gives it an air of authority. I have had companies and job seekers contact me from my listing on Manta.

Finally, ask everyone you connect with for a referral. Referrals have become the core of my business and I always give a nice thank you memento when a referral is hired.

Nineteen Review

!

ⓘ Choose a service to help you stay organized, or develop your own system

ⓘ Utilize LinkedIn

ⓘ Be targeted with social media

ⓘ Join Meet Up groups

ⓘ Join user groups

ⓘ Ask for referrals

ⓘ Reward referrals that are hired

Twenty: All Of The Resources In This Book

!

http://klout.com/home
http://pinterest.com/

http://websearch.about.com/od/internetresearch/a/boolean.htm

http://websearch.about.com/od/internetresearch/a/boolean.htm

http://www.beknown.com/landingBeKnown
http://www.careerjet.com
http://www.Collegegrad.comwww.dice.com
http://www.CollegeRecruiter.comwww.boardex.com
http://www.craigslist.com
http://www.gadball.com

http://www.glassdoor.com

http://www.glassdoor.com

http://www.google.com

http://www.hiredsecrets.com

http://www.indeed.com
http://www.internetinc.com/job-search-websites/ - nursing

http://www.internetinc.com/top-100-job-board-niches/

http://www.jackalopejobs.com/
http://www.jibe.com/
http://www.linkedin.com
http://www.linkup.com

http://www.meetup.com/
http://www.ning.com/
http://www.simplyhired.com
http://www.tweetmyjobs.com/
http://www.twitter.com

http://www.usjobs.com

http://www.watchthatpage.com

http://www.ziggs.com
https://plus.google.com/up/start
https://twitter.com/
https://www.facebook.com
www.aftercollege.com
www.boardex.com
www.careerbuilder.com

www.craigslist.com

www.dice.com

www.efinancialcareers.com

www.FINS.com

www.google.com

www.healthjobsusa.com
www.hoovers.com
www.insideview.com
www.ivyexec.com

www.klout.com

www.mediarecruiter.com

www.monster.com

www.openreqcom

www.spoke.com
www.theladders.com

www.thelistinc.com
www.wikipedia.com

www.wsj.com

www.zoominfo.com
http://jobsover50.com/

http://www.workforce50.com/

http://www.jobs4point0.com/

http://www.retirementjobs.com/

http://www.seniors4hire.org/

http://www.workforce50.com/

http://learnup.me/welcome

BONUS: IS THE GRASS GREENER?
INVESTMENT BANKING VS. PRIVATE EQUITY

!

I left the office early the other day in order to catch the end of my son's high school tennis match. High School tennis is intense (especially when your kid is playing). For the high school tennis team, the reward is winning the match, making it to the play-offs and hopefully winning the league title.

A tennis match is not unlike a corporate finance team at an Investment Bank. They seek to win the right to pitch, make it to the bake-off and secure the engagement. Once they get it they seek to find the buyer or the capital to close the transaction, which, if successful is like winning the league title (especially when it's an IPO like Facebook). Lots of high fives and back slapping, which they hope translate into a lot of money at bonus time.

Whether it's tennis or Investment Banking, we can all agree that winning is great – and when everyone is winning, life is good.

But what happens on the other end? The losing end?

I tend to stand off to the side when I watch my son's matches because I don't want to make him nervous or be tempted to walk up to the fence and tell him to lay his wrist back longer so that he doesn't shank his forehand. If he misses a few forehands in a row, he abandons that shot and begins to run around to hit his two-handed backhand. If his backhand is on that day, you can put money on it that he will hit more backhands than forehands.

What is he doing? He's looking for where the green grass grows. For my son, that would be his backhand.

For an Investment Banker, the greener pasture would be Private Equity.

Over the past two years, I can tell you with certainty that 99.999% of calls and meetings I have had with Investment Bankers always come around to this:

"I'd like to get out of Investment Banking and over to Private Equity. Do you place people in PE?"

"Please help me get into Blackstone."

"I am very secure in my VP role. I will only move for Goldman or Carlyle." FAST FORWARD SIX MONTHS. "Is that opportunity still available?"

"I only see my son ½ hour a day. I am not kidding. I need to move over to the buy-side so I can have a life."

"Dear JB, I will only consider buy-side opportunities: Private Equity, Hedge, VC."

One of the great advantages in my role as a Wall Street Recruiter is that I see trends – long before they become reality.

I knew something was up when even senior revenue producing bankers were asking me if I could get them into Private Equity. Having this question come up in every meeting or phone call meant to me that there was going to be a serious financial shake-out in bonuses in I-Banking.

Welcome to today's reality.

From my perspective, Investment Bankers are looking at the wrong shade of green.

Let's break down why Investment Bankers want to move over to Private Equity.

Based on my hundreds of calls and meetings with so many of them, it comes down to these core reasons:

1.) Stability

2.) Quality of Life

3.) More Money

4.) Prestige

STABILITY

I describe the current state of employment akin to a 'loyal-less society,' meaning there is no job security anymore.

Investment Banks have cycles. They hire big and fire big. Last in/first out, poor performing economy, new management, a trader loses billions for the firm

– whatever the circumstance, there is no loyalty. You ARE expendable AND replaceable.

Are Private Equity firms more stable? Generally, I would say yes. However, the opportunities are smaller because there are less of them. With the new Frank Dodd legislation, I believe we will see even more condensed operations within Private Equity. There are so many compliance issues being required now that PE firms, in my opinion, will not expand.

Additionally, if you are looking to rise up quickly, you might consider another pasture. Once the guys at the top settle in, they are in no hurry to shift firms. Unless, of course, it's Blackstone or their fund runs out of money and they can't raise any more.

Finally, if the fund does not do well, it could close down. Just like that. At least at an Investment Bank there are other divisions that can do well to carry you if the market is not in your favor. AKA: wealth management, retail banking, sales/trading, etc. That is, of course, if you aren't part of the next inevitable RIF at your IB.

QUALITY OF LIFE

By quality of life, I don't just mean living where you want to, but actually being able to *live* outside the four walls of your office.

Many of the firms I recruit people away from require their junior bankers to work 110+ hour weeks. Weekends are not a right, they are a privilege in these tier firms.

Want to get some sun? Buy a sunlamp and install it at your desk.

While life in general at PE firms is quieter, when it's deal crunch time, if you are a junior hire you will be having nightmares of your life as a banker.

The pressure on the leaders to invest well (and junior execs to provide appropriate analysis) is magnified, which could lead to ulcers, pain pill addictions, depression – or maybe looking to where the grass might be growing greener. This could affect your quality of life (aka – stress) because at PE firms, there are only horses. No cows, hens or sheep to help balance the farm.

At my son's tennis match I happened to chat with a Dad who runs a fund for a large corporation (similar to an Intel type fund) that focuses on cross border transactions. The issue they have is such that they can't compete with the big guns (KKR, TPG, Blackstone, etc.) and they don't want to encounter huge risk. So they end up investing in earlier rounds, competing with VC's who have a better pipeline of opportunities.

"We're not making any money at that level," he said. "But I get to watch my son play tennis." So unless you are at the big shops (déjà vu time expectations at junior level), you are at the whim of the ability of the fund to be successful and therefore, need you. Your quality of life could change very quickly.

MORE MONEY

Private Equity salaries are not that different than IB salaries at the lower levels. However, when you reach senior levels such as Managing Director or Partner, then you really begin to participate in the greenery. Think Management Fee and Carried Interest. There are all sorts of pastures to play in.

However, with the green comes the drought. There are often contract clauses that require repayment or hurdle rates that require a certain return on the fund before partners can begin collecting. The pressure to be successful is enormous. If the fund is successful, then even as a junior hire you can do very well. If it is not, no one makes any money.

PRESTIGE

It can be fun to be on the buy-side, especially when the Financial Sponsor Coverage bankers at your old haunt come calling on you. It's fun not to have to beg anymore. However, if you are part of the acquisition or investment decision process, there is a lot of pressure to guess well. If you don't, you could be out. At least in banking you can find another buyer. In PE, if you invest the fund's money and you are wrong – it will be hard for you to find another job.

So what's an Investment Banker to do?

Plant some more fertilizer on his pasture and hope it grows?

Try to get into Private Equity where the grass might not grow any greener?

I think there just may be another way. It is a trend I have been seeing and predicting and whose time, I believe, has finally come.

Investment Bankers might consider migrating to . . .

THE BOUTIQUE INVESTMENT BANK

THE MERCHANT BANK

THE CORPORATE DEVELOPMENT TEAM

THE CONSULTING FIRM

BONUS - COMPANIES

!

The following are a list of leading companies in many industries (in no particular order). They are provided to inspire your thought process on actual companies that you might want to work for. Several industries are included. Look them up, peruse their websites and do a search of their competitors. In doing this you will likely discover companies you had never even thought of applying to, yet which may fit in exactly with your dream job aspirations!

Note: The categories of companies are in random order to encourage free flow association and to spark your imagination.

CONSUMER

!

1-800 Contacts Inc
Agfa Monotype Corporation
Arbonne International LLC
BenQ Corporation
Bose Corporation
Callaway Golf Company
Canon Inc
Casio Inc
Color Kinetics Incorporated
Creative
Creative Technology Ltd.
Crestron Electronics Inc
DiscountContactLenses.com
Dolby Laboratories Inc
DTS , Inc.
Eastman Kodak Company
Electrolux AB
FUJIFILM Corporation
Garmin Ltd.
GNC Corporation
Harman International Industries , Incorporated
Harris Corporation
Hitachi , Ltd.
Hitachi Data Systems Corporation
Home Automation Inc
iBiquity Digital Corporation
InFocus Corporation
JVC Company

K2 Inc.
Konica Minolta Business Solutions Ltd
Kyocera Wireless Corp.
LG Electronics Inc
Matsushita Electric Industrial Co. , Ltd.
Maytag Corp.
Menu Foods , Inc.
Metabo Corporation
Motorola Inc
Nautilus Inc
NBTY , Inc.
Nike , Inc.
Nikon Corporation
Nokia Corporation
Panasonic Corporation
Patagonia Inc
Philips GmbH
Planar Systems Inc
Plantronics , Inc.
Primera Technology , Inc.
RadioShack Corporation
Reckitt Benckiser plc
Ricoh Corporation
Samsung Corporation
Samsung Electronics Co. , Ltd.
Sanyo PLC
Scientific-Atlanta Inc
Sharp Electronics Corporation
Sling Media Inc
Sony Corporation
SRS Labs , Inc.
Syntax-Brillian Corporation
TDK Corporation

The Black & Decker Corporation
The Fuller Brush Company
Thomson Reuters Corporation
TiVo Inc.
Toshiba Corporation
Tyco Electronics Corporation
Unilever N.V.
ViewSonic Corporation
Whirlpool Corporation

Retail

!

Abt Electronics Inc
Acer Inc
American Apparel Inc
American Eagle Outfitters , Inc.
APMEX, Inc
Arrow Electronics , Inc.
Auto Parts GIANT.com
AutoNation Inc
AutoZone Inc.
Barnes & Noble , Inc.
Bass Pro Shops Inc
Bebimi
Best Buy Co. , Inc.
Bjs Wholesale Club Inc
Blockbuster Inc.
CarMax , Inc.
CDW Corporation
Circuit City
Coldwater Creek Inc.
CompUSA , Inc.
Corporate Express , Inc.
CVS Corporation
Dell Inc.
DiscountOfficeSupplies.com
Electronics Boutique
Foot Locker , Inc.
Franci's Flowers Wedding Design
GameFly Inc

GameStop Corp.
GNC Corporation
GoldenMine.com
Harrods Limited
JCPenney Company
Kohl's Corp.
Kroger Co.
Lenovo Group Ltd.
Liz Claiborne Inc.
Lowe's Companies , Inc.
MexGrocer.com LLC
Movie Gallery Inc.
Neiman Marcus
Netflix , Inc.
Newegg Inc
Nordstrom , Inc.
Patagonia Inc
Pep Boys Company
Petco
Premium Outlets I Simon Property
Group
Quiksilver , Inc.
Ray's Canoe Hideaway
Recreational Equipment , Inc.
REI
RhinoSoft
Richemont SA
RONA Inc
Second Time Around Watch Company
Supervalu Inc.
Tech Data Corporation
Teleflora
The Clarks Companies N.A

The Home Depot Inc.
The TJX Companies , Inc.
The White Company
Trans World Entertainment
Corporation
Tweeter Center
United Natural Foods , Inc.
United Rentals , Inc.
Wal-Mart Stores , Inc.
Whole Foods
Wild Oats Markets , Inc.

TELECOMMUNICATIONS

!

Adelphia Communications Corp.
Alltel Corp.
Aplus.Net company
AT&T Inc.
Bandwidth.com Inc
Bell Canada
BellSouth Corporation
British Sky Broadcasting Limited
Broadview Networks Inc
Cable & Wireless plc
Cbeyond , Inc.
China Mobile Ltd.
China Unicom Limited
Cingular Wireless LLC
Clearwire Corporation
Cognigen Networks Inc
Comcast Corporation
ComicGenesis
Covad Communications Group Inc
Cox Communications Inc
DIRECTV Inc
DISH Network L.L.C
EarthLink Inc
Easynet Limited
EchoStar Communications Corporation
Equant N.V.
Eschelon Telecom Inc
Extreme Broadband Sdn. Bhd.

Global Crossing Limited

Globalstar , Inc.

Glowpoint Inc

GoAmerica Communications Corp

Golden Telecom , Inc.

Hostway Corporation

iBasis Inc

Inmarsat plc

Intelsat , Ltd.

Interland , Inc.

Iridium Satellite LLC

Keenspace

KPN N.V.

Level 3 Communications , Inc.

MobilePro Corp.

MobiTV , Inc.

ntl Incorporated

Orange SA

Primus Telecommunications Inc

Q Comm International , Inc.

Qwest Communications International Inc.

RCN Corporation

SAVVIS Inc

Sirius Satellite Radio Inc.

Skype

Speakeasy Inc

Sprint Corp.

T-Mobile Ltd

Telenor AB

Telewest

Telstra Corporation Limited

TELUS Corporation

The Carphone Warehouse Limited
TracFone Wireless Inc
Verizon companies
Verizon Wireless
Vodafone
Vonage
Vonage Holdings Corp.
WorldCom Inc.
XM Satellite Radio Inc
XO Communications Inc

INDUSTRIAL

!

AEROTECH INC
AGCO Corporation
Applied Industrial Technologies Inc
Ariens Company
Art's-Way Manufacturing Co. , Inc.
Atlas Copco AB
Baldor Electric Company
Baldwin Technology Company Inc
BEI Technologies , Inc.
Bobcat Company
Briggs & Stratton Corporation
Buhler Industries Inc
Caterpillar Inc
CNH Global N.V.
CompAir
Cooper Cameron Corporation
Crown Equipment Corporation
Danaher Motion GmbH
Danfoss Inc
Deere & Company
Dresser Inc
Fastenal Co.
Festo Corporation
Flowserve Corporation
Franklin Electric Co. Inc
Gardner Denver Inc
Gehl Company
Generac Power Systems Inc

GlobalSpec Inc
Graco Inc.
Grundfos GmbH
Hardinge Inc.
Husky Injection Molding Systems
Ltd.
Husqvarna AB
Ingersoll-Rand Company
JCB Inc.
JLG Industries Inc
John Deere Limited
Kennametal Inc.
Komatsu America Corp.
Komatsu Ltd.
Kubota Tractor Corporation
Larsen & Toubro Limited
Metso Corporation
Milacron Inc
Multiquip Inc
National Oilwell Varco Inc
NETZSCH Incorporated
NOOK INDUSTRIES INC
Norgren Ltd
Northern Tool & Equipment
Company
NSK Ltd
Parker Hannifin Corporation
Pentair Inc
Regal Beloit Corporation
Rexnord Corporation
Sandvik AB
SKF AB
SPX Corporation

Stewart & Stevenson Services Inc
STIHL Incorporated
Sullair Corporation
Sun Hydraulics Corporation
Swagelok Company
Tecumseh Products Company
Terex Corporation
The Manitowoc Company , Inc.
The Toro Company
TRUMPF Inc
Vermeer Manufacturing Company

MEDIA

!

Adult Friend Finder
America Online , Inc.
Arbitron Inc
BZ/Rights & Permissions , Inc.
CCH INCORPORATED
Celent LLC
ChoicePoint Inc.
Clear Channel Communications , Inc.
Community Newspaper Holdings , Inc.
comScore , Inc.
Datamonitor plc
Der Spiegel
Digg Inc
DisplaySearch LLC
EMI Group PLC
eMusic.com Inc
Equifax Inc.
Experian Ltd
Fig
FindGift.com
Fitch Ratings Ltd
GLOBAL INSIGHT Inc
Golden Horn Records
GoodSearch LLC
HealthGrades , Inc.
IMS Health Incorporated
Information Resources , Inc.
InfoSpace , Inc.

InfoTrends Inc
infoUSA Inc
Inktomi Corporation
INPUT's Federal Agency
Interactive Data Corporation
J.D. Power and Associates Inc
KLAS Enterprises , LLC
Laughing Squid
Law 360
LexisNexis Company
Lionsgate
Lithium Technologies Inc
MediaTec Publishing Inc
Medscape LLC
Mintel
Morningstar, Inc.
New York Daily News
Pixar incorporated
PR Newswire
Reuters Limited
Search Engine Optimization Inc
Solucient LLC
Standard & Poor's
Stratfor
Suite101.com
Technomic Inc.
The Conference Board Inc
The Freedonia Group , Inc.
The Lancet
The McGraw-Hill Companies
The New York Times Company
The Nielsen Company
The NPD Group Inc

The Washington Post Company
TowerGroup Inc.
Trans Union Corporation
Univision Communications Inc.
USA Today
VNU eMedia Inc.
Weiss Ratings , Inc.
Wolters Kluwer nv
Yahoo! Inc

Technology

!

ABB Ltd
Accenture LTD
Adobe
Affiliated Computer Services ,
Inc.
Agile Software Corporation
Akamai Technologies , Inc.
Apple Inc
Autodesk Inc
Automatic Data Processing ,
Inc.
BEA Systems , Inc.
BearingPoint , Inc.
Business Objects SA
Citrix Systems Inc
Cognos Incorporated
Corel Corporation
Documentum , Inc.
Epicor Software Corporation
ESRI Ltd
FileNet Corporation
Fiserv Inc
Hummingbird Ltd
Hyperion Solutions Corporation
IBM Corporation

Informatica Corporation
Intergraph Corporation
Interwoven Inc
KnowledgeStorm Inc
Macrovision Corporation
Microsoft Corporation
MicroStrategy Incorporated
NetIQ Corporation
NetSuite Inc
Open Text Corporation
Oracle Corporation
RealNetworks , Inc.
Red Hat Inc
Salesforce.Com Inc
Silkmoth Ltd
Software AG
Sun Microsystems Inc
Sybase Inc
Symantec Corporation
Synopsys Inc
Tata Consultancy Services Ltd
TIBCO Software Inc
Twitter
UGS Corp.
WebEx Communications Inc
webMethods , Inc.
Websense Inc

REAL ESTATE

Access USA Realty Inc
AEW Capital Management , L.P.
AMB Property Corporation
American Financial Realty Trust
AmREIT Inc
BentleyForbes
Boca Executive Realty LLC
Boston Properties Inc
CB Richard Ellis Inc
Charles Dunn Company
Coldwell Banker Commercial Inc
Coldwell Banker Real Estate Corporation
Coldwell Banker Residential Brokerage
Colliers International Ltd
Colony Capital LLC
CoStar Group , Inc.
CresaPartners LLC
Crescent Resources LLC
Crye-Leike Inc
Cushman & Wakefield Inc
DTZ Holdings plc
ECC Capital Corporation
Emaar Properties
Forest City Enterprises , Inc.
General Growth Properties , Inc.
Grubb & Ellis Company
GVA Worldwide LLC
Hersha Hospitality Trust

Hines
HomeGain.com Inc
Howard Hanna Real Estate Services
Industrial Developments International Inc
Innkeepers USA Trust
Insignia/ESG Inc
Jones Lang LaSalle Incorporated
Keller Williams Realty Inc.
LandAmerica Financial Group Inc
LandAndFarm.com Inc
Lend Lease Corporation
Lexington Corporate Properties Trust
Long & Foster Real Estate Inc
LoopNet , Inc.
Maguire Properties , Inc.
Marcus & Millichap
Merchandise Mart Properties Inc
Mohr Partners Inc
NAI Global Inc
Newmark Knight Frank
NRT Incorporated
Pacific Security Capital Inc
Prudential Northwest Realty Associates
Real Estate Investment Trust
Real Estate.com
Savills plc
Shurgard Storage Centers , Inc.
Sperry Van Ness Inc
Studley Inc
The Corcoran Group Inc
The St. Joe Company
The Staubach Company

The Town and Country Trust
Toll Brothers Inc.
Trammell Crow Company
Transwestern Commercial Services
Transwestern Investment Company ,
L.L.C.
Trizec Properties Inc.
Turnberry International Realty Miami
United Properties , LLC
Weichert Realtors
Windermere Real Estate Services Co

CLOUD COMPUTING

!

3PAR Inc
3Tera , Inc.
4PSA
Abiquo Inc
Advanced Micro Devices , Inc.
Akamai Technologies , Inc.
AMAX Engineering
Corporation
Amazon.com, Inc.
Appistry Inc
Apple Inc
AppNexus Inc
Asigra Inc
Astadia
Cisco Systems Inc
Citrix Systems Inc
DataPipe Inc
DataSynapse Inc
Dell Inc.
Enomaly Inc
FlexiSphere
Google Inc
Hewlett-Packard Company
Hosting.com Inc
Hostway Corporation

IBM Corporation
Intel Corporation
IQity Solutions LLC
Joyent Inc.
Layered Technologies Inc
Meraki Inc
Microsoft Corporation
Model Metrics Inc
NaviSite Inc
NetSuite Inc
Nirvanix
OnLive Inc
OpSource Inc
Penguin Computing Inc
Platform Computing
Corporation
Rackspace Ltd
RightScale Inc
RingCentral Inc
Salesforce.Com Inc
SeeMyRadiology
SGI S.A
Sun Microsystems Inc
Symplified
Verari Systems Inc
VMware , Inc.
Wyse Technology Inc

SOFTWARE

!

Acision
Activision Blizzard
Adobe
Alcatel-Lucent
Ansys
Apple
Aspect Communications
Autodesk
Autonomy
Avid
BMC
CA
Cadence
Capcom
Cegedim Dendrite
Cerner
Check Point
Cisco
Citrix
Compuware
Dassault
Diebold
Electronic Arts
EMC
Epic Systems

Ericsson

ESRI

F5

FICO

Fujitsu

General Electric

Google Inc.

Hitachi

HP

IBM

Infor

Inspur

Intel Corporation

Intergraph

Intuit

Kaspersky Lab

Konami

Lawson

McAfee

McKesson

Mentor Graphics

Microsoft

Misys

Namco Bandai Games

NCR

NetApp >

Nexon Corporation >

Nintendo >

Nokia Siemens
Networks >

Nortel
Novell
Nuance
Open Text
Oracle
Pgi
Philips
Progress
PTC (Parametric)
Qualcomm
Quest
Real
Red Hat
Reynolds & Reynolds
Rockwell Automation
Sage
SAIC
Salesforce.com
SAP
SAS Institute
Sega Sammy Holdings
Shanda Interactive
Siemens
Software AG
Solera Holdings
Sony
Sopra Group
Square Enix
Sterling Commerce
Sun Microsystems
SunGard
Sybase
Symantec

Synopsys
Take Two Interactive
Teradata
Thales Computers
THQ
Totvs
Trend Micro
Ubisoft
Verint
VMWare
Wincor Nixdorf
Wolters Kluwer

NON PROFIT ORGANIZATIONS

!

America's Second Harvest
American Association for the Advancement of Science
American Cancer Society Inc
American Chemical Society
American Civil Liberties Union
American Diabetes Association
American Friends Service Committee
American Library Association
American National Standards Institute
American Public Health Association
American Society for Training and Development
AmeriCares
Amnesty International
Catholic Relief Services
Center for Science in the Public Interest
Children , Inc.
Children's Miracle Network
College Board
Council on American-Islamic Relations
Electronic Frontier Foundation
Electronic Privacy Information Center
Families USA

Global Exchange
Human Rights Watch
Humanity International
Judicial Watch , Inc.
Kaiser Family Foundation
Médecins Sans Frontières
National Assoc. for the Education of Young Children
National Association for the Advancement of Colored People
National Association of Home Builders
National Council of La Raza
National Education Association
National Federation of Independent Business
National Fire Protection Association
National Mental Health Association
National Retail Federation
Natural Resources Defense Council
Public Citizen
Service Employees International Union
Society for Human Resource Management
The ALS Association
The Heritage Foundation
The Leukemia & Lymphoma Society Inc
The Nature Conservancy
The Software & Information Industry Association
The Trust for Public Land
Toastmasters International
World Vision Inc
World Wildlife Fund

Construction

AECOM Technology Corporation

AMEC plc

ARCADIS NV

Arup bv

Balfour Beatty plc

Bechtel Corporation

Black & Veatch Corporation

Bovis Lend Lease Inc

Burns & McDonnell

Camp Dresser & McKee Inc.

Carillion plc

Carter & Burgess Inc

CDM

Ch2M Hill Companies Ltd

DMJM + Harris , Inc.

Earth Tech Inc

EDAW , Inc.

ENSR Corporation

Exponent , Inc.

Fluor Corporation

Gensler

GHD

Golder Associates Ltd.

Halcrow Group Limited

Hatch Ltd

HDR Inc

HNTB Corporation

HOK , Inc.

KBR Inc

Kimley-Horn and Associates , Inc.

Kvaerner PLC

MWH s.a

Parsons Corporation

PBS&J

RBF Consulting

RPS Group Plc

RTKL Associates Inc

Skanska AB

Skidmore , Owings & Merrill LLP

Smith Seckman Reid Inc

SmithGroup Inc

Stantec Inc.

STV Incorporated

Tetra Tech , Inc.

The Louis Berger Group , Inc.

Timmons Group

Turner Construction Company

URS Corporation

Washington Group International Inc

Wilbur Smith Associates , Inc.

BUSINESS SERVICES

!

2Checkout.com , Inc.

Accenture LTD

Affiliated Computer Services , Inc.

Akamai Technologies , Inc.

AMEC plc

America Online , Inc.

American International Group , Inc.

ARAMARK Corporation

Atos Origin S.A

Automatic Data Processing , Inc.

Bain & Company

BearingPoint , Inc.

Business Objects SA

CB Richard Ellis Inc

CCH INCORPORATED

CGI Group Inc

Citigroup Inc

Computer Sciences Corporation

Cushman & Wakefield Inc

Deloitte LLP

DIRECTV Inc

EDS Corporation

Ernst & Young LLP

Halliburton Company
Hewitt Associates LLC
Jones Lang LaSalle Incorporated
JPMorgan Chase & Co.
Keane , Inc.
KeyCorp
McKesson Corporation
Netflix , Inc.
PricewaterhouseCoopers LLP
Rentokil Initial plc
Sapient Corporation
Satyam Computer Services Ltd.
Schlumberger Limited
Shutterfly Inc
Sodexho Inc
Software AG
SYNNEX Corporation
Tata Consultancy Services Ltd
The Hackett Group Inc
TIAA-CREF
TIBCO Software Inc
Unisys Corporation
USAA
webMethods , Inc.
Wells Fargo & Co.
Wolters Kluwer nv
WPP Group plc

AIRLINES

!

Aer Lingus Limited
Air Asia
Air Canada
Air Charter Service Inc
Air China Limited
Air France
Air India
Air New Zealand Limited
AirTran Airways Inc
Alaska Airlines Inc
Allegiant Air , LLC
ALOHA AIRLINES INC
America West Airlines Inc
American Airlines , Inc.
ATA Airlines , Inc.
Atlas Air Worldwide Holdings Inc
BAA plc
British Airways
China Southern Airlines Company
Limited
Continental Airlines Inc
Delta Air Lines Inc
easyJet plc
Emirates
Etihad Airways

Executive Jet Management Inc

Flight Options LLC

Flybe Limited

Hawaiian Airlines Inc

Indian Airlines Limited

International Lease Finance Corporation

JetBlue Airways Corporation

KLM

Logan Airport

Lufthansa AG

Malaysia Airlines

Mesaba Airlines

NetJets Inc.

Northwest Airlines Corp.

O'Hare International Airport

PrivatAir SA

Prive Jets

Qantas

Qatar Airways Ltd

Ryanair

Singapore Airlines

Southwest Airlines Co.

United Air Lines Inc

US Airways Inc

WestJet

Wizz Air

CONSULTING

ABT Solutions Ltd
Accenture
Acutest Ltd
All Covered Inc
Analysts International Corporation
Appshop Inc
Avineon Inc
Baseline Consulting Group Inc
Blue Star Infotech Ltd
BORN Inc
Bristlecone Inc
Business & Decision Ltd
C3i Inc
Caneum Inc
Cap Gemini Ernst & Young LLC
Cap Gemini SA
CGI Group Inc
Cognizant Technology Solutions
Corporation
DataLogic International , Inc.
Delinea Corporation
Deloitte Consulting
Dyncorp Inc.
eLoyalty Corporation
ESYNC

eVergance Partners LLC

Extraprise

First Consulting Group Inc

Foliage Software Systems Inc

GeoAnalytics , Inc.

Gestalt LLC

Healthlink Incorporated

IBM Global Services

ICICI OneSource Limited

Infogain Corporation

Infosys Technologies Ltd.

Infotech Enterprises Ltd

ITNET plc

Logic Software , Inc.

Logical

NCI Information Systems , Inc.

neoIT.com Inc

NerveWire Inc

Outsourcing Solutions Inc.

R Systems INC

RIS Inc

Shinetech

Sierra Systems Group Inc

Sonata Software Limited

TechTeam Global , Inc.

Trianz Inc

Vistronix Inc

Zallas Technologies Inc

ADVERTISING

!

Aberdeen Group Inc
Advanstar Communications Inc
ADVO , Inc.
APCO Worldwide Inc
aQuantive , Inc.
Arbitron Inc
BI WORLDWIDE
Brodeur Worldwide
Cone , Inc.
Dataquest Inc.
Decision Analyst Inc
Digitas Inc
Direct Response Technologies Inc
DoubleClick Inc.
Edelman Inc
EDGE3 Corporation
Federal Sources , Inc.
Fleishman-Hillard Inc
Forrester Research , Inc.
Frost & Sullivan
Gartner , Inc.
GfK AG
iCrossing Inc
IDC Company
IDG WORLD EXPO CORP
In-Stat companies
Infonetics Research Inc

InfoTrends Inc
InsightExpress LLC
Interactive Inc
Ipsos S.A
JupiterResearch
Ketchum Inc
Landor Associates
Line Drive Marketing
Maritz Inc.
Merkle Inc
META Group , Inc.
Millward Brown , Inc.
Modem Media Ltd
MWW Group Inc
Ogilvy & Mather
Omnicom Group Inc.
Organic , Inc.
Ovum Ltd
Parks Associates
Penton Media , Inc.
Publicis Groupe S.A.
Ruder Finn , Inc.
Slack Barshinger
Synovate Limited
Technology Marketing Corporation
Technomic Inc.
The Kelsey Group Inc
The Nielsen Company
The Phelps Group
The Radicati Group , Inc.
TNS
ValueClick Inc
Venture Development Corporation

VerticalResponse , Inc.
Vertis Inc
VISIT FLORIDA Inc
VNU eMedia Inc.
Web Ad.vantage Inc
Weber Shandwick Company
Witeck-Combs Communications , Inc.
Yankee Group
Yankelovich , Inc.
Young & Rubicam Inc.

GRAPHIC DESIGN

!

2Advanced Studios LLC
Acro Media Inc
Aleven Music Marketing & Design
Arch Creative Group
Artest Design Group
Blue Water Media LLC
Brainfusion Studios Inc
Brand Identity Guru Inc
Corey McPherson Nash
Coudal Partners
Creative Source Design Group Inc
CyberMotion
Daigle Design Inc
Design Hovie Studios Inc
Design Junction Pty Ltd
Design Studios , LLC
Distinction Limited
Dynamic Digital Advertising LLC
Fluidesign
Formula Design
Grantastic Designs Inc
Gsinc Ltd
Hornall Anderson Design Works Inc
ImageWorks Studio Ltd
IQLogo

Karen Spencer Design Inc

Landor Associates

Logo Design Guru Inc

Logo Design Works Company

LogoBee Inc

Logoworks

Lunatrix Design Ltd

One Pica , Inc.

OtherWisz Creative Corporation

Phinney/Bischoff Design House

Pixellogo

RainCastle Communications Inc

Sideburn Studios

Sleepless Media

Society for Environmental Graphic
Design

Specto Design Inc

StockLayouts LLC

Symbiotic Design

THAT Agency LLC

The Logo Company

The Logo Factory Inc

theGrafixGuy LLC

TradeMark Media Corporation

Viaden Inc

Web Design Company

STAFFING

!

Adecco SA
Administaff , Inc.
Ajilon LLC
AMN Healthcare Inc
Aquent Inc
BrassRing LLC
Buck Consultants , Inc.
CareerBuilder , Inc.
Cejka Search Inc
Ceridian Corporation
Challenger , Gray & Christmas Inc.
Chandler Hill Partners Inc
Christian & Timbers Inc
ComputerJobs.com Inc
Convergys Corporation
DBM Inc
DHR International Inc
Dice Inc.
ExecuNet Inc
Gray & Christmas Inc.
Hay Group Inc
Heidrick & Struggles , Inc.
Heidrick & Struggles International Inc
Hewitt Associates LLC
HotJobs.com , Ltd.

InteliStaf.com Corporation

Kelly Services Inc

Kenexa Corporation

Kforce Inc

Korn/Ferry International Inc.

Lee Hecht Harrison LLC

Lucas Group Company

Management Recruiters International Inc

Manpower Inc

MRINetwork

OfficeTeam

Paychex , Inc.

Personnel Decisions International
Corporation

Russell Reynolds

Robert Half International Inc.

Robert Half Technology

Spencer Stuart

Spherion Corporation

The Creative Group

The Segal Company

TheraKare Inc

TMP Worldwide Inc.

Towers Perrin

Watson Wyatt Worldwide, Inc.

William M. Mercer Inc.

Yoh Services LLC

FILM & ENTERTAINMENT

!

800.COM Inc.
Amazon.com, Inc.
Arrow Distributing Company
Baker & Taylor , Inc.
Best Buy Co. , Inc.
Blockbuster Inc.
Borders Group , Inc.
Borders Inc
BrainPOP.com LLC
Bravo Productions Inc
British Sky Broadcasting Limited
Buy.com Inc.
Circuit City
CleanFilms.com
Cobra Video LLC
CompUSA , Inc.
Dreamworks Animation Skg, Inc.
Excalibur Films
GameZnFlix , Inc.
Grizzly Adams Productions Inc
Hallmark Channel
Handleman Company
Hearst Communications Inc.
Hip Interactive Corp.
IGN PC

J&R Electronics Inc

LodgeNet Entertainment Corporation

Movies

MPI Media Group

Musicland Group Inc.

Netflix , Inc.

Nordisk Film

Pixar Animation Studios Inc.

Platinum Distribution

PorchLight Entertainment Inc

Primesco Inc.

RHI Entertainment , Inc.

Saavn

Spyglass Entertainment

Swank Motion Pictures , Inc.

Tai Seng

The Walt Disney Company

TightFit Productions

TLA Video

Trans World Entertainment
Corporation

Turner Classic Movies Inc

Turner Entertainment Co.

Urban Christian Entertainment

Vivid Entertainment LLC

Women Make Movies , Inc.

TRAVEL AND TOURISM

!

Accor SA
American Hockey League
Bally Total Fitness Corporation
Betfair
BetUS Company
Bluegreen Corporation
Bodog
Brinker International Inc
California Pizza Kitchen Inc
Chick-fil-A , Inc.
Choice Hotels International Inc
Comfort Inn
Crowne Plaza Hotel
Darden Restaurants Inc.
Doubletree Hotel
Ecruise
Embassy Suites Hotel
Fairmont Hotel
FelCor Lodging Trust Incorporated
Four Seasons Hotels Limited
Hampton Inn
Harrahs Entertainment Inc
Hilton Hotels Corporation
Holiday Inn
Hyatt Corporation

InterContinental Hotels
Interstate Hotels & Resorts Inc
Intrawest Corporation
Major League Baseball
Marriott International Inc
Microgaming
National Football League
National Hockey League
O'Charley's Inc
PinnacleSports.com
Prime Sites USA LLC
Radisson Hotel
Radisson SAS Hotels & Resorts
RealTime Gaming
Red Robin
Regal Entertainment Group
ResortQuest
Sportingbet PLC
Sportsbook
Starwood Hotels & Resorts Worldwide ,
Inc.
Station Casinos Inc
The Cheesecake Factory Incorporated
The Ritz-Carlton
Troon Golf LLC
Wynn Las Vegas LLC

TRANSPORTATION

!

Air Van Moving Company
Alstom SA
American Commercial Lines Inc.
American Moving and Storage
Association
AmeriCold Logistics LLC
BDP International Inc
Brocade Communications Systems , Inc.
Center for Neighborhood Technology
Compania Logistica de Hidrocarburos
Computer Network Technology
Corporation
Delphi Corporation
Dunbar Armored , Inc.
Eimskip BV
Enbridge Energy Partners , L.P.
Enbridge Inc.
Follett Corporation
Hatch Ltd
Hitachi , Ltd.
HK Systems , Inc.
IBM Corporation
Invensys plc
Iron Mountain Incorporated
Kinder Morgan , Inc.

Kinder Morgan Energy Partners , L.P.

Kinder Morgan Management LLC

Kirby Corporation

Menlo Worldwide LLC

Momart Ltd

ONEOK , Inc.

ONEOK Partners , L.P.

Pacer International , Inc.

Parsons Corporation

Plains All American Pipeline , L.P.

Questar Pipeline Company

Recall Corporation

Ryder System, Inc.

TECO Transport

Teekay Shipping Corporation

The Bekins Company

The Brink's Company

Thule Inc

Transco plc

TransMontaigne Partners L.P.

Trinity Industries Inc

Union Gas Limited

United Van Lines LLC

URS Corporation

Versacold Corporation

Wallenius Wilhelmsen Logistics

William B. Meyer Inc

NATURAL RESOURCES

!

AGL Resources Inc.
American Museum of Natural
History
Anadarko Petroleum Corporation
Anglo American plc
BG Group plc
BHP Billiton Ltd.
Burlington Resources Inc.
Canadian Natural Resources
Limited
Caterpillar Inc
CCH INCORPORATED
CenterPoint Energy Inc
Chesapeake Energy Corporation
Cliffs Natural Resources Inc.
Crosstex Energy , L.P.
Deltic Timber Corp
EnCana Corporation
Enogex Inc.
ENTRIX Inc
EOG Resources , Inc.
EXCO Resources , Inc.
Exxon Mobil Corporation
Garcia and Associates
GEORESOURCES INC

Jones & Stokes

Linn Energy LLC

MDU Resources Group Inc

Natural Resources Defense Council

NiSource Inc.

Odwalla Inc.

Penn Virginia Corp

Pepco Holdings Inc

PetroFalcon Corporation

Questar Corp

Quicksilver Resources Inc.

Sherritt International Corporation

Software AG

Spectra Energy Corp

Swift Energy Company

Teck Cominco Limited

Tesoro Petroleum Corp.

The Doe Run Company

The Williams Companies Inc

Unico , Incorporated

Unocal Corp.

Us Energy Corp

Vectren Corporation

W&T Offshore , Inc.

Whole Foods Market Inc

Xcel Energy Inc.

Xstrata plc

FITNESS

!

24 Hour
Alpha Fitness Equipment
Apex Fitness Group Inc
Aphelion Inc
Bally Total Fitness Corporation
Body Works Fitness Equipment , Inc.
Club One Inc
Contours Express LLC
Curves
Curves International Inc
Diet-Fat-Loss.net
Equinox Fitness Club
Esporta
Fitcorp
Fitness First Company
Fitness First Limited
Fitness Together
GlobalFit
Gold's Gym Inc
healthclubs.casinohq.net
healthclubs.city-sleuth.com
healthclubs.coincity.net
healthclubs.cpaguild.net
healthclubs.docguild.net
healthclubs.healthyandrich7.com

healthclubs.make-money7.com

Healthtrax Inc

Healthworks

Holmes Place

IM=X Pilates Studios

Jazzercise Inc

LA Boxing

LA Fitness

LA Fitness

LIFE TIME FITNESS Inc

LivingWell

Los Angeles Athletic Club

New York Athletic Club

New York Sports Club

Power Systems Inc

Seattle Athletic Club

ShapeXpress Inc

Snap Fitness Inc

Stroller Strides LLC

The Sports Club/LA

Town Sports International Holdings , Inc.

Town Sports International Holdings Inc

Washington Athletic Club

Wellbridge Athletic Club

YouBeFit.com

HEALTHCARE SERVICES

!

Accenture LTD
American International Group , Inc.
AmerisourceBergen Corporation
Amn Healthcare Services Inc
Apria Healthcare Group Inc.
APS Healthcare Inc
ARAMARK Corporation
Baxter International Inc
Cardinal Health Inc
Cejka Search Inc
Computer Sciences Corporation
Consorta Inc
Covansys Corporation
Covidien Ltd.
EDS Corporation
Ernst & Young LLP
Gambro AB
GlaxoSmithKline plc
HCA Inc.
HCIA Inc.
HealthGrades , Inc.
Hewitt Associates LLC
Hythiam , Inc.
InteliStaf.com Corporation
Johnson & Johnson

Joint Commission on Accreditation of Healthcare
Organizations
JPMorgan Chase & Co.
Kindred Healthcare Inc
Manhattan Research LLC
McKesson Corporation
MED3OOO Inc
Merge eFilm Inc
Misys Healthcare Systems Inc
Misys plc
Novation , LLC
Novo Nordisk Inc
Novo Nordisk Inc
PricewaterhouseCoopers LLP
Roche
Satyam Computer Services Ltd.
SmithKline Beecham Corporation
Sodexho Inc
Solucient LLC
SYNNEX Corporation
Tata Consultancy Services Ltd
Universal Health Services , Inc.
VCA Antech , Inc.
Wells Fargo & Co.
Wolters Kluwer nv
WPP Group plc

Life Sciences

!

Advanced Life Sciences
Holdings , Inc.
Afexa Life Sciences Inc
Affinity Life Sciences Inc
AIBMR Life Sciences , Inc.
Amorfix Life Sciences Ltd.
Apollo Life Sciences Ltd
Arkion Life Sciences LLC
Arysta LifeScience Corporation
Arysta LifeScience North America
Corporation
BIOCRATES Life Sciences AG
Bioniche Life Sciences Inc.
Boston Life Sciences , Inc.
Caliper Life Sciences Inc
CK Life Sciences Int'l. Inc
ColBar LifeScience Ltd
Enzo Life Sciences Inc
Excel Life Sciences , Inc.
GangaGen Life Sciences Inc.
GenoLogics Life Sciences

Software Inc.

Huntingdon Life Sciences

IABG Life Sciences Solutions
GmbH

IBC Conferences Ltd.

IBC USA Conferences , Inc.

Innova LifeSciences
Corporation

Integra LifeSciences
Corporation

International Council for the Life
Sciences

International Life Sciences
Institute

Ithaka Life Sciences Ltd

ITI Life Sciences

Life Lab Science Program

Life Science Analytics Inc

LifeScience Alley

LifeScience-Consulting , Inc.

LifeSpan BioSciences , Inc.

MediChem Life Sciences , Inc.

Meridian Life Science Inc

MVM Life Science Partners LLP

Nanobac Pharmaceuticals , Inc.

NAPROD Life Sciences

NEN Life Science Products , Inc.

Ottawa Life Sciences Council

PerkinElmer Life Sciences , Inc.

Pittsburgh Life Sciences
Greenhouse Inc
Precept Life Sciences
Precerche Life Sciences , LP
Prevalere Life Sciences , Inc.
ProMetic Life Sciences Inc.
Provida Life Sciences Inc
Provista Life Sciences LLC
QBI Life Sciences Inc
RBC Life Sciences Inc
RTS Life Science
SeraCare Life Sciences , Inc.
Strand Life Sciences
Suven Life Sciences Limited
Tepnel Life Sciences PLC
Xanthus Pharmaceuticals , Inc.

AUTOMOTIVE

!

AUDI AG
Azure Dynamics Corporation
Ballard Power Systems Inc.
Chrysler LLC
Club Car Inc.
Cummins Inc
Daimler AG
DaimlerChrysler AG
Detroit Diesel Corporation
Ducati
E-Z-GO
Edmunds.com Inc
Enova Systems Inc
Fleetwood Enterprises , Inc.
Fleetwood RV
Ford Motor Company
Freightliner LLC
Fuji Heavy Industries Ltd.
General Motors Corp.
Harley-Davidson , Inc.
Hino Motors Ltd.
Honda S.A
Hyundai Motor Company
International Truck and Engine

Corporation
ISE Corporation
Iveco Ltd
Jaguar
Land Rover Ltd
Lexus incorporated
Mack Trucks Inc.
Mahindra & Mahindra Ltd.
Monaco Coach Corporation
Navistar International Corporation
Oshkosh Truck Corporation
PACCAR Inc
Polaris Industries Inc
Porsche AG
Prodrive Limited
Renault SA
Ricardo plc
Saturn Corporation
Scania AB
Suzuki Corporation
Tesla Motors Inc
The Subaru Limited
Toyota PLC
Volkswagen AG
Volvo AB
Westport Innovations Inc.
ZAP , Inc.

Restaurants

!

Applebee's IP LLC
Applebee's Neighborhood Grill & Bar
Arby
Baja Fresh
Benihana Inc
Bonefish Grill
Boston Market Corporation
Boston Pizza
BUCA , Inc.
Burger King
California Pizza Kitchen Inc
Caribou Coffee Company , Inc.
Champps Entertainment Inc.
Checkers Drive-In Restaurants , Inc.
Chez Panisse
Chick-fil-A , Inc.
Chili's
CKE Restaurants , Inc.
Corner Bakery Cafe
Del Taco Inc
Diedrich Coffee Inc
Domino's Pizza LLC
Dunkin' Donuts Incorporated
El Pollo Loco , Inc.
HMSHost Corporation
IHOP Corp.
Il Fornaio Corporation
Jack in the Box Inc

Jollibee
KFC Corporation
Landry's Restaurants , Inc.
Legal Sea Foods Inc
Lettuce Entertain You Enterprises , Inc.
Levy Restaurants
McCormick & Schmicks Seafood Restaurants Inc.
Metromedia Restaurant Group
Noodles & Company
O'Charley's Inc
Olive Garden Company
Osi Restaurant Partners, Inc.
Outback Steakhouse Inc
P.F. Chang
Panda Express
Peet's Coffee & Tea , Inc.
Pizza Hut Inc
Quiznos
RARE Hospitality International Inc
Red Lobster
Restaurant Associates
Rock Bottom Restaurants , Inc.
Rubio's Restaurants Inc
Ruby Tuesday Inc
Ruth's Chris
Sbarro Inc
Schlotzsky's , Inc.
Sheetz Inc.
Souper Salad
Starbucks Corporation
Subway
T.G.I. Friday

Taco Bell Corp.
Taco Bueno
Taco Del Mar Corporation
The Coffee Bean
The Krystal Company
The Lavazza company
The Melting Pot
Tricon Global Restaurants , Inc.
Van Houtte Inc
Wienerschnitzel

APPAREL

Abercrombie & Fitch Co.
Aeropostale , Inc.
American Apparel Inc
American Eagle Outfitters , Inc.
AnnTaylor Stores Corporation
Blair Corporation
Bluefly , Inc.
Brookstone , Inc.
Casual Male Retail Group , Inc.
Charming Shoppes , Inc.
Coldwater Creek Inc
Columbia Sportswear Company
Crocs Inc.
Cutter & Buck Inc.
Dillard's Inc.
eBags Inc
Eddie Bauer , Inc.
Esprit
Foot Locker , Inc.
Gap Inc.
Genesco Inc.

Guess? , Inc.

Hot Topic , Inc.

J. Crew

Jones Apparel Group , Inc.

Kellwood Company

L.L. Bean , Inc.

Lands' End Inc

Lillian Vernon Corporation

Linens 'n Things , Inc.

Liz Claiborne Inc.

Marks and Spencer plc

Matalan PLC

Nordstrom Inc

Patagonia Inc

Payless ShoeSource , Inc.

Quiksilver , Inc.

SKECHERS USA , Inc.

Talbots Inc.

The Buckle , Inc.

The Finish Line , Inc.

The J. Jill Group , Inc.

The Timberland Company

The TJX Companies , Inc.

The White Company

Under Armour, Inc.

Urban Outfitters Inc

VF Corporation

Williams-Sonoma , Inc.

Zappos.com Inc

SEMICONDUCTORS

!

Advanced Micro Devices , Inc.

Agere Systems Inc

Altera Corporation

Analog Devices Inc

Applied Materials , Inc.

Atheros Communications , Inc.

Atmel Corporation

AuthenTec Inc

Broadcom Corporation

California Micro Devices Corporation

Cirrus Logic Inc.

Conexant Systems , Inc.

Cree Inc

CSR plc

Denali Software , Inc.

Diodes Incorporated

EMCORE Corporation

Fairchild Semiconductor Ltd

Freescale Semiconductor , Inc.

Hynix Semiconductor Inc.

IDT Inc

Infineon Technologies AG

Intel Corporation

Intersil Corporation

Lattice Semiconductor Corporation

Linear Technology Corporation

LSI Logic Corporation

Metalink Ltd.

Microchip Technology Inc.

Microsemi Corporation

Microtune Inc

MIPS Technologies , Inc.

National Semiconductor Corporation

NVIDIA Corporation

PMC-Sierra Inc

Rambus Inc.

Ramtron International Corporation

RF Micro Devices , Inc.

Semtech Corporation

SigmaTel , Inc.

Skyworks Solutions Inc

Spansion Inc.

STMicroelectronics N.V.

Synplicity , Inc.

Taiwan Semiconductor Manufacturing Company

Texas Instruments Incorporated

VIA Technologies , Inc.

WJ Communications , Inc.

Xilinx Inc

Zoran Corporation

PRIVATE EQUITY

!

Accel Partners BV
Accel-KKR LLC
Acumen Fund Inc
Advanced Technology Ventures
Advent International Corporation
Alta Partners
Apax Partners , L.P.
Atlas Venture GmbH
Austin Ventures LP
Bain Capital LLC
Battery Ventures L.P
Benchmark Capital Companies
Burrill & Company
Canaan Partners LP
ComVentures
Doughty Hanson & Co
Draper Fisher Jurvetson
Elevation Partners
Fenway Partners , Inc.
Foundation Capital
Francisco Partners LP
Frontenac Company
Garage Technology Ventures LLC
General Atlantic Partners , LLC
Genstar Capital , LLC
Greylock Partners
Gryphon Investors Inc
GTCR Golder Rauner , LLC

H.I.G. Capital LLC
Hellman & Friedman LLC
Hercules Technology Growth Capital , Inc.
Ignition Partners , LLC
In-Q-Tel Inc
Intersouth Partners
InterWest Partners LLC
Kleiner Perkins Caufield & Byers
Kohlberg Kravis Roberts & Co.
KRG Capital Partners LLC
Madison Dearborn Partners LLC
Maveron LLC
Mayfield Fund
Mohr Davidow Ventures
Morgenthaler Ventures
New Enterprise Associates Ltd.
North Castle Partners LLC
Norwest Venture Partners
Nth Power LLC
Oxford Bioscience Partners
Parthenon Capital LLC
Perseus LLC
Providence Equity Partners Inc.
Sequoia Capital
Silver Lake Partners
SJF Ventures Limited
Sofinnova Ventures Inc
Sprout Group
Summit Partners Limited
Sun Capital Partners , Inc.
TA Associates Inc
Technology Crossover Ventures
Texas Pacific Group

Thoma Cressey Equity Partners Inc.
Trident Capital
Vector Capital Corporation
Ventures West Management Inc.
Vestar Capital Partners Inc
vSpring Capital
Walden International
Warburg Pincus LLC
Wind Point Partners

DEFENSE

!

Airbus
ARINC Incorporated
Armor Holdings Inc
ATK incorporated
B/E Aerospace , Inc.
BAE Systems Inc.
Bell Helicopter
Bombardier Inc.
CAE Inc.
Cessna Aircraft Company
Cubic Corporation
DRS Technologies Inc
EADS N.V
EDO Corporation
Elbit Systems Ltd.
Embraer S.A
Emrise Corporation
FlightSafety International Inc
General Atomics Aeronautical Systems ,
Inc.
General Dynamics Corporation
General Electric Company
GKN Plc
Goodrich Corporation
Gulfstream Aerospace Corporation

Honeywell International Inc

International Launch Services

ITT Corporation

L-3 Communications Corporation

Lockheed Martin Corporation

Northrop Grumman Corporation

Orbital Sciences Corporation

Pratt & Whitney

QinetiQ Ltd

Raytheon

Rockwell Collins Inc

Rolls-Royce plc

Sikorsky Aircraft Corporation

SMITHS AEROSPACE LLC

Snecma SA

SPACEHAB , Incorporated

Taser International Inc.

Teledyne Technologies Incorporated

Textron Inc.

Thales SA

The Boeing Company

TRW Automotive

United Defense Industries , Inc.

United Technologies Corp.

UQM TECHNOLOGIES , INC.

WÃ¤rtsilÃ¤ Corporation

Legal Services

!

Akin Gump Strauss Hauer & Feld LLP

Allen & Overy LLP

Alston & Bird LLP

Arnold & Porter LLP

Baker & McKenzie LLP

Baker Botts L.L.P.

Brinks Hofer Gilson & Lione

Chadbourne & Parke LLP

Dechert LLP

DLA Piper LLP

Duane Morris LLP

Earthjustice

Eversheds LLP

Fenwick & West LLP

Fisher & Phillips LLP

Foley & Lardner LLP

Freshfields Bruckhaus Deringer LLP

Fulbright & Jaworski L.L.P.

Goodwin Procter LLP

Greenberg Traurig LLP

Hogan & Hartson LLP

Holland & Knight LLP

Hunton & Williams LLP

Jackson Lewis LLP

Jones Day

Kirkland & Ellis LLP
Latham & Watkins LLP
Lieff Cabraser Heimann & Bernstein
LLP
Linklaters LLP
Littler Mendelson P.C
Lovells LLP
Mayer Brown Rowe & Maw LLP
McDermott Will & Emery LLP
Media Access Project
Morgan , Lewis & Bockius LLP
Nixon Peabody LLP
Norton Rose Limited
Perkins Coie LLP
Pillsbury Winthrop LLP
Proskauer Rose LLP
Reed Smith LLP
Seyfarth Shaw LLP
Sidley Austin LLP
Simmons & Simmons
Thomas More Law Center
Vinson & Elkins LLP
Weil , Gotshal & Manges LLP
White & Case LLP
Wilson Sonsini Goodrich & Rosati ,
P.C.
Winston & Strawn LLP

Investment Banking

!

ABN AMRO Ltd
ABRY Partners LLC
AdMedia Partners , Inc.
American Capital
Apollo Management , L.P.
BlackRock Inc
Blackstone Group LP
BMO Financial Group
BNP Paribas Limited
Cantor Fitzgerald LP
Castle Harlan , Inc.
Cerberus Capital Management LP
Chase
Citi
Clayton , Dubilier & Rice , Inc.
Credit Suisse First Boston LLC
CVC Capital Partners
Davidowitz & Associates Inc.
Deutsche Bank AG
Dresdner Kleinwort Wasserstein Limited
Duff & Phelps , LLC
Edward Jones Limited
Fortress Investment Group LLC
Frank Russell Company
Golden Gate Capital Inc
Goldman , Sachs & Co.
Gores Technology Group LLC
Greenhill & Co. , Inc.

Houlihan Lokey Howard & Zukin Inc
Investcorp S.A.
Janney Montgomery Scott
JMPG
J.P. Morgan & Co.
Jefferies & Company , Inc.
Keefe , Bruyette & Woods , Inc.
Lazard Ltd
Legg Mason , Inc.
LPL Financial Services
Macquarie Bank Limited
Mellon
Merrill Lynch & Co. Inc
Merriman Curhan Ford & Co.
Morgan Keegan & Co.
Morgan Stanley & Co.
Needham & Company , Inc.
Northern Trust Corporation
Permira Limited
Piper Jaffray & Co.
Platinum Equity LLC
Rabobank
Robertson Stephens & Co.
Salomon Smith Barney Inc.
Sandler O'Neill & Partners , L.P.
Schroders plc
Securities Investor Protection Corporation
SEI Investments Company
Smith Barney , Inc.
State Street Corporation
Stifel , Nicolaus & Company , Incorporated
The Bear Stearns Companies Inc.
The Carlyle Group

The Northwestern Mutual Wealth Management
Company
ThinkEquity Partners LLC
Thomas H. Lee Partners , L.P.
Thomas Weisel Partners LLC
U.S. Trust Corporation
UBS AG
Veronis Suhler Stevenson LLC
Wedbush Morgan Securities , Inc.
William Blair & Co.
Wilshire Associates Incorporated
Yucaipa Cos.

Venture Capital

Accel Partners BV

Advent International Corporation

Apax Partners , L.P.

Bain Capital , LLC

Battery Ventures L.P

Draper Fisher Jurvetson

Garage Technology Ventures LLC

General Atlantic Partners , LLC

GTCR Golder Rauner , LLC

H.I.G. Capital LLC

Hellman & Friedman LLC

In-Q-Tel Inc

Kleiner Perkins Caufield & Byers

Madison Dearborn Partners LLC

New Enterprise Associates Ltd.

Providence Equity Partners Inc.

Sequoia Capital

Silver Lake Partners

Summit Partners Limited

Sun Capital Partners , Inc.

TA Associates Inc

Texas Pacific Group

Trident Capital

Warburg Pincus LLC

Wind Point Partners

Advanced Technology Ventures

Benchmark Capital Companies

Burrill & Company

Canaan Partners LP

Doughty Hanson & Co

Francisco Partners LP

Genstar Capital , LLC

Greylock

Hercules Technology Growth Capital , Inc.

Ignition Partners , LLC

Intersouth Partners

InterWest Partners LLC

Mayfield Fund

Morgenthaler Ventures

Nth Power LLC

Atlas Venture GmbH

Austin Ventures LP

Oxford Bioscience Partners

Perseus LLC

Thoma Cressey Equity Partners Inc.

Ventures West Management Inc.

vSpring Capital

Walden International

BONUS – CHANGING CAREERS

!

Go back to Chapters Two and Three with your dream job hat on. What do you really want to do? Have you taken the assessment tests to see what you might be best suited for?

I remember taking a personality likes/dislikes test in high school that spit out which careers I might enjoy and be good at. They were: Talk Show Host, Sales, Public Relations, Actress and Coach. As I think back on my career path, I have filled all of these roles, with the most fulfilling of all being a Career Coach to job seekers.

Here are a few more tests that you can enroll if you still have no idea what your dream job is. Have some fun – you might be surprised at what careers these tests suggest!

http://www.mycareerquizzes.com/career-personality-tests

http://www.quizrocket.com/career-personality-test

http://www.quibblo.com/quiz/7MgqRmi/Which-Job-Suits-You

You can also conduct searches with your ideal job parameters, although this might not be as targeted.

Search profiles on LinkedIn for similar job characteristics or industries that you might be interested in. Review the current and past companies that those professionals have worked at. This is an excellent way to see how others have followed their career and or changed.

If you know what career you would like to change to, you must start your search with that in mind. Craft your C.V. to included characteristics that support the new role you intend to have.

Reach out to colleagues, industry executives and your social network to find those that are currently in the kind of job you wish to have and connect with them. Learn from them and thank them for their perspective.

Volunteer at an organization that is related to the industry that you may want to change to. We learn by doing and in doing, you may gain a clearer picture of your path.

Consider enrolling in a class or skills based program that will help you prepare for your new role. For example, let's say you are in sales but you want to do voiceovers. Enroll in a voice training class, develop a demo and send it to local talent agencies in your community.

Maybe you are in consulting, yet you wish to be a sports coach. Volunteer to be an assistant coach for a local school sports team and learn from the coach in charge.

I know a Media Executive who became a Realtor. He took the training courses at night, applied for his license and joined a small firm. After three years in his new role, he is one of the top producers in his community.

I know a Wealth Management Professional who went off on his own to raise money for international recycling companies. He started small and now is onto his fifth capital raise.

I know a Realtor who wanted to be an Actress. She took acting classes, put together a headshot and short résumé and convinced an agency to take her on. She now does commercials, print ads and acts in local community theatre.

I know an Investment Banker who wanted to be a CEO of a technology start-up. He parlayed his finance experience into the role by agreeing to raise capital for the company as their CFO. Within six months he was named CEO and is very happy.

I know a Roofing Contractor who wanted to build homes. He took several architecture courses at the local community college, volunteered with a local architect on weekends and has since built his first home and sold it for a nice profit.

I know the President of a theme park engineering company who wanted to be Mayor of her town. At the time of this publishing she is in the midst of running a great campaign.

Look at what you do now. Go through the process described earlier in this book and identify your dream job. Take your current skills and craft them into the position of your dreams. Search for others in the role(s) you desire. Reach out to them. Learn from them. Contact companies in the field you wish to enter. Meet with employees, learn from them and always thank everyone for their time and input.

You may have to enlist in more schooling, you may have to volunteer or you could even work for free (although for high level roles this does not always transfer as valuable). Do what it takes. Stay focused with determination and persistence. It will happen for you if you don't waver, regardless of bumps along the way.

The Author of this book is living proof of what it takes to change careers and to never give up.

BONUS – JOBS FOR THE BOOMER GENERATION

!

My Father always told me that when he retired, he wanted to be a greeter at WalMart. He got close to that by working for the Post Office delivering mail. In his affable, jovial way, he was a regular greeter to everyone on his mail route. He loved it!

Many Baby Boomer job seekers are afraid because they think that there are no jobs for the over 50 crowd. If you are a Baby Boomer, I am here to tell you that you are wrong!

It is true that sometimes this generation of professionals is overlooked because the impression is that they may not be as flexible with work demands. After all, they have already put in their time. I am sure this does not refer to you. Other companies may think that this group is too expensive or are over qualified, not to mention the objection that you simply are too old.

In today's challenging economy it is important to be open to opportunity in whatever form it presents itself. Don't be wedded to only one type of job or career. Be open to the world and see what might fit you at this stage in your career.

Many Baby Boomers have to work because the economy has raided their savings and the cost of living has gone up more than they anticipated. If this is your situation, do not panic.

Here are some ways that you can explore new opportunities:

1. Join your local S.C.O.R.E. chapter. Make yourself available to mentor younger start-ups or growing businesses that may require your expertise. I know a senior executive who was pushed out of the job force and through S.C.O.R.E. and similar mentoring organizations, has landed on three Boards of Directors. He is making a nice stipend and has stock in the companies. The best part of all – his advice is valued and he feels as though he is contributing to the next generation of successful entrepreneurs.

2. Team up with extension programs that are set up to help the Baby Boomer workforce. http://www.empowered.com/ is a career counseling organization that is focused on this demographic.

3. Education: Go to your local Community College and brush up on a skill that can parlay into a lasting position. Adult Extension courses are also offered in the evenings at most Community Colleges. Another way you can educate yourself is to acquire new skills according to particular job requirements. Learn Up is a new site that will help you learn those skills and then update your experience so that you fill the requirements for listed roles. This is also a

good source for any job seeker who would like to improve their skill set. http://learnup.me/welcome.

4. Be a flex worker. Fill in when someone is on leave or be the 'go to' executive that does not require full benefits. Being an Independent Contractor can be lucrative in any field.

Do not be discouraged. America is aging, the retirement age is increasing and every company needs wisdom and experience in the ranks. The right job is there for you.

Here are some special portals that you can search for positions that may fit your profile.

http://jobsover50.com/

http://www.workforce50.com/

http://www.jobs4point0.com/

http://www.retirementjobs.com/

http://www.seniors4hire.org/

http://www.workforce50.com/

Be positive and persistent. You will succeed!

Thank you for reading HIRED!
You are prepared to secure your dream job!
I look forward to hearing of your success!

- J.B. Miller

JB Miller is the President of C2C Executive Search, a national Executive Search firm. She has written this book so that every job seeker has practical, applicable advice to help them get HIRED!

Articles by JB Miller

COVER LETTER!
The secret formula for making yours stand out

CV!
More than a Resume

GET THE INTERVIEW!
How to jump to the top of the resume pile

APPLYING TO A JOB POSTING!
Where does my resume go?

"JB prepared me for the job of my dreams. I am now the Head of East Coast Sales for a leading technology company."
– Senior Sales Executive

"JB knows exactly what kind of candidate we need."
– Head of Investment Banking Firm

"By following the ideas in this book, you will be ahead of the competition."
– Just hired Vice President, New York